TABLE OF CONTENTS

Secret Key #1 - Time is Your Greatest Enemy

Pace Yourself

Wear a watch. At the beginning of the test, check the time (or start a chronometer on your watch to count the minutes), and check the time after every few questions to make sure you are "on schedule."

If you are forced to speed up, do it efficiently. Usually one or more answer choices can be eliminated without too much difficulty. Above all, don't panic. Don't speed up and just begin guessing at random choices. By pacing yourself, and continually monitoring your progress against your watch, you will always know exactly how far ahead or behind you are with your available time. If you find that you are one minute behind on the test, don't skip one question without spending any time on it, just to catch back up. Take 15 fewer seconds on the next four questions, and after four questions you'll have caught back up. Once you catch back up, you can continue working each problem at your normal pace.

Furthermore, don't dwell on the problems that you were rushed on. If a problem was taking up too much time and you made a hurried guess, it must be difficult. The difficult questions are the ones you are most likely to miss anyway, so it isn't a big loss. It is better to end with more time than you need than to run out of time.

Lastly, sometimes it is beneficial to slow down if you are constantly getting ahead of time. You are always more likely to catch a careless mistake by working more slowly than quickly, and among very high-scoring test takers (those who are likely to have lots of time left over), careless errors affect the score more than mastery of material.

Secret Key #2 - Guessing is not Guesswork

You probably know that guessing is a good idea - unlike other standardized tests, there is no penalty for getting a wrong answer. Even if you have no idea about a question, you still have a 20-25% chance of getting it right.

Most test takers do not understand the impact that proper guessing can have on their score. Unless you score extremely high, guessing will significantly contribute to your final score.

Monkeys Take the Test

What most test takers don't realize is that to insure that 20-25% chance, you have to guess randomly. If you put 20 monkeys in a room to take this test, assuming they answered once per question and behaved themselves, on average they would get 20-25% of the questions correct. Put 20 test takers in the room, and the average will be much lower among guessed questions. Why?

1. The test writers intentionally writes deceptive answer choices that "look" right. A test taker has no idea about a question, so picks the "best looking" answer, which is often wrong. The monkey has no idea what looks good and what doesn't, so will consistently be lucky about 20-25% of the time.
2. Test takers will eliminate answer choices from the guessing pool based on a hunch or intuition.

Simple but correct answers often get excluded, leaving a 0% chance of being correct. The monkey has no clue, and often gets lucky with the best choice.

This is why the process of elimination endorsed by most test courses is flawed and detrimental to your performance- test takers don't guess, they make an ignorant stab in the dark that is usually worse than random.

$5 Challenge

Let me introduce one of the most valuable ideas of this course- the $5 challenge:

You only mark your "best guess" if you are willing to bet $5 on it.
You only eliminate choices from guessing if you are willing to bet $5 on it.

Why $5? Five dollars is an amount of money that is small yet not insignificant, and can really add up fast (20 questions could cost you $100). Likewise, each answer choice on one question of the test will have a small impact on your overall score, but it can really add up to a lot of points in the end.

The process of elimination IS valuable. The following shows your chance of guessing it right:

If you eliminate wrong answer choices until only this many answer choices remain:	Chance of getting it correct:
1	100%
2	50%
3	33%

However, if you accidentally eliminate the right answer or go on a hunch for an incorrect answer, your chances drop dramatically: to 0%. By guessing among

all the answer choices, you are GUARANTEED to have a shot at the right answer.

That's why the $5 test is so valuable- if you give up the advantage and safety of a pure guess, it had better be worth the risk.

What we still haven't covered is how to be sure that whatever guess you make is truly random. Here's the easiest way:

Always pick the first answer choice among those remaining.

Such a technique means that you have decided, **before you see a single test question**, exactly how you are going to guess- and since the order of choices tells you nothing about which one is correct, this guessing technique is perfectly random.

This section is not meant to scare you away from making educated guesses or eliminating choices- you just need to define when a choice is worth eliminating. The $5 test, along with a pre-defined random guessing strategy, is the best way to make sure you reap all of the benefits of guessing.

Secret Key #3 - Practice Smarter, Not Harder

Many test takers delay the test preparation process because they dread the awful amounts of practice time they think necessary to succeed on the test. We have refined an effective method that will take you only a fraction of the time.

There are a number of "obstacles" in your way to succeed. Among these are answering questions, finishing in time, and mastering test-taking strategies. All must be executed on the day of the test at peak performance, or your score will suffer. The test is a mental marathon that has a large impact on your future.

Just like a marathon runner, it is important to work your way up to the full challenge. So first you just worry about questions, and then time, and finally strategy:

Success Strategy

1. Find a good source for practice tests.
2. If you are willing to make a larger time investment, consider using more than one study guide- often the different approaches of multiple authors will help you "get" difficult concepts.
3. Take a practice test with no time constraints, with all study helps "open book." Take your time with questions and focus on applying strategies.
4. Take a practice test with time constraints, with all guides "open book."
5. Take a final practice test with no open material and time limits

If you have time to take more practice tests, just repeat step 5. By gradually exposing yourself to the full rigors of the test environment, you will condition your mind to the stress of test day and maximize your success.

Secret Key #4 - Prepare, Don't Procrastinate

Let me state an obvious fact: if you take the test three times, you will get three different scores. This is due to the way you feel on test day, the level of preparedness you have, and, despite the test writers' claims to the contrary, some tests WILL be easier for you than others.

Since your future depends so much on your score, you should maximize your chances of success. In order to maximize the likelihood of success, you've got to prepare in advance. This means taking practice tests and spending time learning the information and test taking strategies you will need to succeed.

Never take the test as a "practice" test, expecting that you can just take it again if you need to. Feel free to take sample tests on your own, but when you go to take the official test, be prepared, be focused, and do your best the first time!

Secret Key #5 - Test Yourself

Everyone knows that time is money. There is no need to spend too much of your time or too little of your time preparing for the test. You should only spend as much of your precious time preparing as is necessary for you to get the score you need.

Once you have taken a practice test under real conditions of time constraints, then you will know if you are ready for the test or not.

If you have scored extremely high the first time that you take the practice test, then there is not much point in spending countless hours studying. You are already there.

Benchmark your abilities by retaking practice tests and seeing how much you have improved. Once you score high enough to guarantee success, then you are ready.

If you have scored well below where you need, then knuckle down and begin studying in earnest. Check your improvement regularly through the use of practice tests under real conditions. Above all, don't worry, panic, or give up. The key is perseverance!

Then, when you go to take the test, remain confident and remember how well you did on the practice tests. If you can score high enough on a practice test, then you can do the same on the real thing.

General Strategies

The most important thing you can do is to ignore your fears and jump into the test immediately- do not be overwhelmed by any strange-sounding terms. You have to jump into the test like jumping into a pool- all at once is the easiest way.

Make Predictions

As you read and understand the question, try to guess what the answer will be. Remember that several of the answer choices are wrong, and once you begin reading them, your mind will immediately become cluttered with answer choices designed to throw you off. Your mind is typically the most focused immediately after you have read the question and digested its contents. If you can, try to predict what the correct answer will be. You may be surprised at what you can predict.

Quickly scan the choices and see if your prediction is in the listed answer choices. If it is, then you can be quite confident that you have the right answer. It still won't hurt to check the other answer choices, but most of the time, you've got it!

Answer the Question

It may seem obvious to only pick answer choices that answer the question, but the test writers can create some excellent answer choices that are wrong. Don't pick an answer just because it sounds right, or you believe it to be true. It MUST answer the question. Once you've made your selection, always go back and check it against the question and make sure that you didn't misread the question, and the answer choice does answer the question posed.

Benchmark

After you read the first answer choice, decide if you think it sounds correct or not. If it doesn't, move on to the next answer choice. If it does, mentally mark that answer choice. This doesn't mean that you've definitely selected it as your answer choice, it just means that it's the best you've seen thus far. Go ahead and read the next choice. If the next choice is worse than the one you've already selected, keep going to the next answer choice. If the next choice is better than the choice you've already selected, mentally mark the new answer choice as your best guess.

The first answer choice that you select becomes your standard. Every other answer choice must be benchmarked against that standard. That choice is correct until proven otherwise by another answer choice beating it out. Once you've decided that no other answer choice seems as good, do one final check to ensure that your answer choice answers the question posed.

Valid Information

Don't discount any of the information provided in the question. Every piece of information may be necessary to determine the correct answer. None of the information in the question is there to throw you off (while the answer choices will certainly have information to throw you off). If two seemingly unrelated topics are discussed, don't ignore either. You can be confident there is a relationship, or it wouldn't be included in the question, and you are probably going to have to determine what is that relationship to find the answer.

Avoid "Fact Traps"

Don't get distracted by a choice that is factually true. Your search is for the answer that answers the question. Stay focused and don't fall for an answer that is true but incorrect. Always go back to the question and make sure you're choosing an answer that actually answers the question and is not just a true statement. An answer can be factually correct, but it MUST answer the question asked. Additionally, two answers can both be seemingly correct, so be sure to read all of the answer choices, and make sure that you get the one that BEST answers the question.

Milk the Question

Some of the questions may throw you completely off. They might deal with a subject you have not been exposed to, or one that you haven't reviewed in years. While your lack of knowledge about the subject will be a hindrance, the question itself can give you many clues that will help you find the correct answer. Read the question carefully and look for clues. Watch particularly for adjectives and nouns describing difficult terms or words that you don't recognize. Regardless of if you completely understand a word or not, replacing it with a synonym either provided or one you more familiar with may help you to understand what the questions are asking. Rather than wracking your mind about specific detailed information concerning a difficult term or word, try to use mental substitutes that are easier to understand.

The Trap of Familiarity

Don't just choose a word because you recognize it. On difficult questions, you may not recognize a number of words in the answer choices. The test writers don't put "make-believe" words on the test; so don't think that just because you only recognize all the words in one answer choice means that answer choice must be correct. If you only recognize words in one answer choice, then focus on that one. Is it correct? Try your best to determine if it is correct. If it is, that is

great, but if it doesn't, eliminate it. Each word and answer choice you eliminate increases your chances of getting the question correct, even if you then have to guess among the unfamiliar choices.

Eliminate Answers

Eliminate choices as soon as you realize they are wrong. But be careful! Make sure you consider all of the possible answer choices. Just because one appears right, doesn't mean that the next one won't be even better! The test writers will usually put more than one good answer choice for every question, so read all of them. Don't worry if you are stuck between two that seem right. By getting down to just two remaining possible choices, your odds are now 50/50. Rather than wasting too much time, play the odds. You are guessing, but guessing wisely, because you've been able to knock out some of the answer choices that you know are wrong. If you are eliminating choices and realize that the last answer choice you are left with is also obviously wrong, don't panic. Start over and consider each choice again. There may easily be something that you missed the first time and will realize on the second pass.

Tough Questions

If you are stumped on a problem or it appears too hard or too difficult, don't waste time. Move on! Remember though, if you can quickly check for obviously incorrect answer choices, your chances of guessing correctly are greatly improved. Before you completely give up, at least try to knock out a couple of possible answers. Eliminate what you can and then guess at the remaining answer choices before moving on.

Brainstorm

If you get stuck on a difficult question, spend a few seconds quickly brainstorming. Run through the complete list of possible answer choices. Look at each choice and ask yourself, "Could this answer the question satisfactorily?" Go through each answer choice and consider it independently of the other. By systematically going through all possibilities, you may find something that you would otherwise overlook. Remember that when you get stuck, it's important to try to keep moving.

Read Carefully

Understand the problem. Read the question and answer choices carefully. Don't miss the question because you misread the terms. You have plenty of time to read each question thoroughly and make sure you understand what is being asked. Yet a happy medium must be attained, so don't waste too much time. You must read carefully, but efficiently.

Face Value

When in doubt, use common sense. Always accept the situation in the problem at face value. Don't read too much into it. These problems will not require you to make huge leaps of logic. The test writers aren't trying to throw you off with a cheap trick. If you have to go beyond creativity and make a leap of logic in order to have an answer choice answer the question, then you should look at the other answer choices. Don't overcomplicate the problem by creating theoretical relationships or explanations that will warp time or space. These are normal problems rooted in reality. It's just that the applicable relationship or explanation may not be readily apparent and you have to figure things out. Use your common sense to interpret anything that isn't clear.

Prefixes

If you're having trouble with a word in the question or answer choices, try

dissecting it. Take advantage of every clue that the word might include. Prefixes and suffixes can be a huge help. Usually they allow you to determine a basic meaning. Pre- means before, post- means after, pro - is positive, de- is negative. From these prefixes and suffixes, you can get an idea of the general meaning of the word and try to put it into context. Beware though of any traps. Just because con is the opposite of pro, doesn't necessarily mean congress is the opposite of progress!

Hedge Phrases

Watch out for critical "hedge" phrases, such as likely, may, can, will often, sometimes, often, almost, mostly, usually, generally, rarely, sometimes. Question writers insert these hedge phrases to cover every possibility. Often an answer choice will be wrong simply because it leaves no room for exception. Avoid answer choices that have definitive words like "exactly," and "always".

Switchback Words

Stay alert for "switchbacks". These are the words and phrases frequently used to alert you to shifts in thought. The most common switchback word is "but". Others include although, however, nevertheless, on the other hand, even though, while, in spite of, despite, regardless of.

New Information

Correct answer choices will rarely have completely new information included. Answer choices typically are straightforward reflections of the material asked about and will directly relate to the question. If a new piece of information is included in an answer choice that doesn't even seem to relate to the topic being asked about, then that answer choice is likely incorrect. All of the information needed to answer the question is usually provided for you, and so you should not have to make guesses that are unsupported or choose answer choices that require unknown information that cannot be reasoned on its own.

Time Management

On technical questions, don't get lost on the technical terms. Don't spend too much time on any one question. If you don't know what a term means, then since you don't have a dictionary, odds are you aren't going to get much further. You should immediately recognize terms as whether or not you know them. If you don't, work with the other clues that you have, the other answer choices and terms provided, but don't waste too much time trying to figure out a difficult term.

Contextual Clues

Look for contextual clues. An answer can be right but not correct. The contextual clues will help you find the answer that is most right and is correct. Understand the context in which a phrase or statement is made. This will help you make important distinctions.

Don't Panic

Panicking will not answer any questions for you. Therefore, it isn't helpful. When you first see the question, if your mind goes blank, take a deep breath. Force yourself to mechanically go through the steps of solving the problem and using the strategies you've learned.

Pace Yourself

Don't get clock fever. It's easy to be overwhelmed when you're looking at a page full of questions, your mind is full of random thoughts and feeling confused, and the clock is ticking down faster than you would like. Calm down and maintain the pace that you have set for yourself. As long as you are on track by monitoring your pace, you are guaranteed to have enough time for yourself. When you get to the last few minutes of the test, it may seem like you won't have enough time left, but if you only have as many questions as you should have left at that point, then you're right on track!

Answer Selection

The best way to pick an answer choice is to eliminate all of those that are wrong, until only one is left and confirm that is the correct answer. Sometimes though, an answer choice may immediately look right. Be careful! Take a second to make sure that the other choices are not equally obvious. Don't make a hasty mistake. There are only two times that you should stop before checking other answers. First is when you are positive that the answer choice you have selected is correct. Second is when time is almost out and you have to make a quick guess!

Check Your Work

Since you will probably not know every term listed and the answer to every question, it is important that you get credit for the ones that you do know. Don't miss any questions through careless mistakes. If at all possible, try to take a second to look back over your answer selection and make sure you've selected the correct answer choice and haven't made a costly careless mistake (such as marking an answer choice that you didn't mean to mark). This quick double check should more than pay for itself in caught mistakes for the time it costs.

Beware of Directly Quoted Answers

Sometimes an answer choice will repeat word for word a portion of the question or reference section. However, beware of such exact duplication – it may be a trap! More than likely, the correct choice will paraphrase or summarize a point, rather than being exactly the same wording.

Slang

Scientific sounding answers are better than slang ones. An answer choice that begins "To compare the outcomes…" is much more likely to be correct than one that begins "Because some people insisted…"

Extreme Statements

Avoid wild answers that throw out highly controversial ideas that are proclaimed as established fact. An answer choice that states the "process should used in certain situations, if…" is much more likely to be correct than one that states the "process should be discontinued completely." The first is a calm rational statement and doesn't even make a definitive, uncompromising stance, using a hedge word "if" to provide wiggle room, whereas the second choice is a radical idea and far more extreme.

Answer Choice Families

When you have two or more answer choices that are direct opposites or parallels, one of them is usually the correct answer. For instance, if one answer choice states "x increases" and another answer choice states "x decreases" or "y increases," then those two or three answer choices are very similar in construction and fall into the same family of answer choices. A family of answer choices is when two or three answer choices are very similar in construction, and yet often have a directly opposite meaning. Usually the correct answer choice will be in that family of answer choices. The "odd man out" or answer choice that doesn't seem to fit the parallel construction of the other answer choices is more likely to be incorrect.

Top 20 Test Taking Tips

1. Carefully follow all the test registration procedures
2. Know the test directions, duration, topics, question types, how many questions
3. Setup a flexible study schedule at least 3-4 weeks before test day
4. Study during the time of day you are most alert, relaxed, and stress free
5. Maximize your learning style; visual learner use visual study aids, auditory learner use auditory study aids
6. Focus on your weakest knowledge base
7. Find a study partner to review with and help clarify questions
8. Practice, practice, practice
9. Get a good night's sleep; don't try to cram the night before the test
10. Eat a well balanced meal
11. Know the exact physical location of the testing site; drive the route to the site prior to test day
12. Bring a set of ear plugs; the testing center could be noisy
13. Wear comfortable, loose fitting, layered clothing to the testing center; prepare for it to be either cold or hot during the test
14. Bring at least 2 current forms of ID to the testing center
15. Arrive to the test early; be prepared to wait and be patient
16. Eliminate the obviously wrong answer choices, then guess the first remaining choice
17. Pace yourself; don't rush, but keep working and move on if you get stuck
18. Maintain a positive attitude even if the test is going poorly
19. Keep your first answer unless you are positive it is wrong
20. Check your work, don't make a careless mistake

Theoretical & Knowledge Bases of Reading

Process of reading

Three stages of reading

Children gain literacy through emergent, beginning and fluent stages. The emergent stage is marked by children noticing environmental print, showing interest in books, pretending to read and using picture cues and predictable patterns in books in order to retell a story. They also can identify some letters, reread books with patterns that are predictable and recognize up to 10 familiar words. The beginning stage will show the child identifying letter names and sounds, match written and spoken words, use the beginning, middle and ending sounds to decode words, recognize as many as 100 high-frequency words, read slowly, word by word, and self-correct while they are reading. The fluent stage features automatic identification with most words, reading with expression, reading at about 100 words per minute or more, preferring to read silently, recognizing up to 300 high-frequency words, often reading independently making inferences.

Form function of oral language

The form function of oral language consists of phonology, morphology and syntax. Phonology is the system of phonemes or sounds in language. Morphology is the system of rules governing word structure and organization. There are many sounds that have no meaning by themselves and these are phonemes but all morphemes have meanings that are either on their own or as root words, or by being attached to a root word such as a prefix, suffix, or word ending. In English, the normal sentence is structured as subject + verb + object. Syntax refers to the way words are combined into sentences. Students with an understanding of syntax can comprehend how the various parts of a sentence relate to each other.

Morphology

Morphology is a sub-discipline of linguistics, or the study of word structure. Words are accepted as being the smallest syntactical units but in most languages words can be related to other words by rules. Those who speak English can recognize these relationships can be formulated as rules applying to many other pairs of words. For example, fire is to firefighter, as cow is to cowboy. Morphology is the linguistic branch that studies such rules across and within languages. Common usage of the word "word" is ambiguous. For example, "cat" and "cats." In one sense the two are the same word and in another they are different words. The distinction between these two senses is one of morphology's most important ones. The first sense of "word" the one in which cat and cats are the same word is called lexeme. The second sense is called word form.

It is possible to distinguish between two kinds of morphological rules. Some rules relate different forms of the same lexeme. Other rules relate two lexemes that are different. Rules that relate to the different forms are called inflectional rules. Those rules relating to two lexemes are word formation rules. The plural for dog, dogs, is an inflectional rule. Compounds such as cowboy or firefighter are word formation rule examples. Word formation informally forms new words while inflection provides more forms of the same word. A distinction also exists between two kinds of word formation, derivation and compounding. Compounding involves combining complete word forms into compounds. Derivation involves prefixes or suffixes that are not independent words.

The concept of a paradigm is closely related to inflection. The paradigm of a lexeme is the set of all of its word forms and is organized by their grammatical categories. Examples of paradigms include verb conjugation or declensions of nouns. Word forms of lexemes can normally be arranged into tables and classified by shared features that include tense, aspect, number, case, gender or mood. Categories that are used to group word forms into paradigms cannot be chosen arbitrarily and must be categorized relevant to syntactic rules. The main difference between word formation and inflection is that inflectional forms are organized into paradigms which are defined by requirements of syntactic rules. The area of morphology dealing with that relationship is called morphosyntax and it is related to inflection and paradigms but not compounding or word inflection.

The one-on-one correspondence between meaning and form hardly ever holds in language and this is one of the largest sources of complexity in morphology. There are words in English such as deer/deer, goose/geese where the differences between singular and plural forms are signaled differently from a regular pattern or are not at all signaled. Even the cases considered normal are not that simple. For example, consider that the -s in cats and the -s in doges are not pronounced the same way. In plural like dishes there is another vowel before the -s. The cases where the same distinction is affected by different changes of form for different lexemes are known as allomorphy. The study of allomorphy resulting from the interaction of

morphology and phonology is called morphophonology.

Three different families of approaches to morphology attempt to capture the distinctions in different ways. They are morpheme based morphology, lexeme-based morphology and word-based morphology. Morpheme-based morphology is where word forms are analyzed as sequences of morphemes, or the minimal meaningful unit of language. Words such as independently have in-, depend, -ent, and -ly as morphemes with the root word being depend. The other morphemes are derivational affixes, or morphemes that attach to words. In words such as cats, cat is the root and -s is an inflectional morpheme. Analyzing word forms as if they were composed of morphemes that are put after each other like a string of pearls is called "item and arrangement morphology."

Lexeme-based morphology is normally an "item and process morphology." Rather than analyzing word forms as sets of morphemes that are arranged in sequence, the word form is a result of applying rules that alter word form or stems to produce new ones. An inflectional rule takes a stem, makes changes to it and out puts a word form. Unlike the item and process approach, the item and arrangement process, one may take a word such as geese and not need to consider it a zero-morph. Instead, while the plural of cat is made by adding an -s to the end of the word, the plural of goose is made by changing the vowel stem.

Word-based morphology is considered a word and paradigm approach to morphology. This theory takes paradigms as a central notion. Rather than stating rules to combine morphemes into word forms, or generate word forms from stems, word-based morphology has generalizations that hold between inflectional paradigm forms. A main point behind this approach is that many generalizations are hard to state with either morpheme-based or lexeme-based morphology. An example is where a piece of a word is given. In a morpheme-based theory it would be called an inflectional morpheme and correspond to a combination of grammatical categories. A word and paradigm approach treats these as whole words related to one another through analogy rules.

Lexical affixes

Lexical affixes, also known as semantic affixes, are elements that are bound and appear as affixes but function as incorporated nouns within verbs and as elements of compound nouns. In other words, they are similar to word roots or stems in function but are similar to affixes in form. Although they are similar to incorporated nouns, lexical affixes differ in that they never occur in freestanding nouns. They always appear as affixes. Such affixes are a relative rarity. Lexical suffixes often show little or no resemblance to free nouns with similar meaning. When used, lexical suffixes usually have a more general meaning. A language has a lexical suffix which means water in a general sense. However it might not have a noun equivalent referring to water in general and has several nouns with more specific meanings, such as saltwater or groundwater.

Orthography

The orthography of a language refers to the set of rules of how to write correctly in the writing system of a language. The term comes from the Greek ortho-, meaning correct, and graphos meaning "that writes." In the modern sense of the word this includes spelling and punctuation. Orthography includes the writing system of a language. For instance, English has 26 letters in an alphabet for both consonants and vowels but no glyph, or specific symbols that represent a semantic or phonetic unit of definitive value in a writing system, for emphasis. But each letter in the English alphabet may represent more than one sound and each sound may be written by more than one letter, "f" and "ph," for example. Orthography entails certain rules on how letters are used such as "i before "e" except after c."

Acquisition and understanding terms

The following terms associated with the acquisition and understanding of language:
Grapheme - a letter or combination of letters in the written language which represents a meaningful sound (phoneme) in the spoken language.
Syntax – the rules which govern the grammatical relationship between words and other units within a sentence.
Grammar – rules for syntax, inflection and word formation which govern how sentences are formed.
Semantics – the study of linguistic meaning in a language, including words, phrases, and sentences. 5. Dialect – a language variation occurring in a certain region or social class; differs from the standard language in pronunciation, grammar or vocabulary.
Syntactic hierarchy: The syntactic hierarchy from smaller to larger units is morpheme, word, phrase, sentence and text.
Syntactic processing: Syntactic processing involves the ability to identify clauses, noun phrases, verb phrases, prepositional phrases, adjectives, articles, nouns and verbs and assemble them in sentence that are syntactically acceptable.
Syntactic development: Syntactic development is measured by the mean length of utterance which is based on the average length of a child's sentences that are scored on transcripts of spontaneous speech. Each unit of meaning is recorded which include root words and inflections.

Sometime after the second year after a child has about 50 words in his or her vocabulary, multiple word utterances begin to appear. These are usually telegraphic and normally without articles, propositions or other grammatical modifications.

Four systems of language

Before a child enters school, he has already developed language at home. Language is defined as a system of expressing and taking in information in a meaningful way. Speech is the verbal expression of language. Four language systems have been identified:

- Phonological (sound) system – refers to the meaningful sounds of a language (phonemes) and their corresponding letters of the alphabet.
- Syntactic (structural) system – refers to the structural organization (grammar) of a language which dictates how words are combined into sentences; components of syntax include word order, capitalization, punctuation and morphemes.
- Semantic (meaning) system – refers to vocabulary, including synonyms, antonyms, and idioms.
- Pragmatic (social & cultural) system – refers to the social and cultural aspects of usage, such as how language varies among different social classes, ethnic groups, and geographic areas.

The Phonological, or sound, system of language refers to the meaningful sounds of a language and their corresponding letters. The meaningful sounds are called phonemes. There are approximately 44 phonemes in the English language. By the time a child is four or five years old, he should be saying most sounds correctly. A grapheme is a letter or combination of

letters in the written language which represents a phoneme in the spoken language. In the English language, a phoneme is often represented by more than one grapheme. For example, the word "thin" has four graphemes (t-h-i-n) but only three phonemes (th-i-n). The combination "th" is considered a digraph, where two letters represent one sound.

Phonological terms:
The following are terms associated with the sounds of language:

- Phonological awareness - a conscious sensitivity to the structure of language by sound. It includes the ability of distinguishing between parts of speech such as syllables and phonemes.
- Phonemic awareness - a part of phonological awareness in which listeners may understand and distinguish between phonemes.
- Alphabetic principle - an assumption that underlies systems of alphabetic writing that each speech sound or phoneme of a particular language requires its own distinctive representation graphically.
- Decoding - willingness and ability to sound out words through generation of sounds into recognizable words, known as a phonological recording.

The Syntactic, or structural, system of language refers to the structural organization (grammar) of a language which dictates how words are combined into sentences. Components of syntax include word order, capitalization and punctuation. Children apply these rules when creating simple, compound and complex sentences. By the time a child is four or five, he will utilize the same grammar as other family members. Another component of the Syntactic system is morphemes, which are the smallest units of meaning. The individual parts of a morpheme mean nothing on their own. For example, the word "thin" is a single morpheme made up of four graphemes (t-h-i-n) and three phonemes (th-i-n).

The Semantic, or meaning, system of language refers to vocabulary, including synonyms, antonyms, and figurative speech. By the time a child enters school, he should have a vocabulary of approximately 5,000 words. During the elementary grades, the child will add another 3,000 words a year. The growth achieved through reading and through other areas of the curriculum. In the Semantic system, figurative speech, such as idioms, can be particularly difficult for young learners or for people new to a language. In the case of idioms, a phrase is used to mean something quite different from the individual words. Idioms usually originate in one group, and then spread to more general usage.

The following are semantic terms:
- Semantic property - contains the components of a word's meaning. For example, female is a semantic property of girl, woman, waitress, etc.
- Semantic class - contains words sharing a semantic property. Semantic classes can intersect. Female and young can be a girl.
- Semantic feature - a notational method that may be used to express whether semantic properties exist or do not exist by using a plus or minus sign.
- Semantic change - the change in one meaning of a word. Each word has a variety of connotations and senses which can be removed, added, or altered over time. Sometimes it is to the extent that words of a particular

time period mean something very different than the same words from a previous time.
- Semantic progression - the evolution of word usage, normally to where the original meaning is very different from its original usage.

Phonemic awareness

Different levels of phonemic awareness in terms of abilities include:
- Hearing rhymes and alliteration as measured by knowing nursery rhymes.
- To do tasks such as comparing and contrasting the sounds of words for rhyme and alliteration, also known as oddity tasks.
- Blending and splitting syllables.
- Performing phonemic segmenting such as counting out the number of phonemes contained in a word.
- Performing tasks of phoneme manipulation such as adding or deleting a particular phoneme.

Instruction in phonemic awareness might include:
- Engaging preschool children in activities directing their attention to sounds in words such as rhyming games.
- Teaching segmentation and blending.
- Coming letter-sound relationship instruction with segmentation and blending.
- Sequence examples systematically when teaching blending and segmentation.

Phonemic awareness is difficult because:
- There are about 40 phonemes or sound units in the English language despite their being 26 letters in the alphabet.

- There are 250 different spellings representing sounds such as "f" as in "ph" or "gh."
- Phonemes, or sound units, are not necessarily obvious. They must be taught. The sounds that make up words are not distinctly separate from each other, also known as "coarticulated." Additionally, phonemes such as "fat" and "hat" are said to have different phonemes "f" and "h" in English despite little difference in sound to distinguish the words. These are called a "minimal pair." If no minimal pair are found to demonstrate two distinct sounds, these sounds may be "allophones." Allophones are variant sounds not recognized by a speaker as distinct and are not significantly different in language so they are looked upon as being the same.

Children of kindergarten age require development of phonemic awareness by hearing, identifying and manipulating phonemes or individual sounds within spoken words. Once children acquire knowledge of letters, they can be taught to perform activities to isolate phonemes and achieve phoneme segmentation by pointing to or manipulating letters along with sounds. Blending and segmentation in phonemic awareness is important because they provide foundation for skills such as spelling. Studies have shown phonemic awareness can be acquired with instruction of 20 hours or less although some children might require more instruction in order to accurately segment words. The individual students should be assessed to verify that the instruction was successful. More instruction might be required for some children more than others.

Phonological recoding

Phonological recoding refers to the use of systematic relationships between letters and phonemes in order to produce the pronunciation of a printed string that is unknown or to spell words. Phonological recoding includes regular word reading, irregular word reading and advanced word analysis. Regular word reading includes beginning recoding such as the ability to read from left to right words that are regular and unfamiliar, generation of sounds for letters and blending sounds into recognizable words. Beginning spelling is translating speech to print through phonemic awareness. Irregular word reading is reading those words that cannot be decoded because either the letter sounds are unique to the word or a few words or the letter-sound correspondences in the word have not yet been learned. Advanced word analysis is knowing those words needed for fluency.

Phonics

The Phonics approach teaches reading and spelling in a methodical fashion by emphasizing the basic relationships between symbols and sounds. These relationships are then applied to words as a way of discerning their meaning. Phonics is an approach often used with beginning readers or with people who are new to a language. The Phonics approach relies heavily on repetitive drills to teach students consonants, vowels and how some letters blend together. Students then take the next step of combining individual sounds into words. Phonics teaches students to recognize unfamiliar words by breaking them down into smaller, more recognizable letter-sound groupings. As students advance, however, research shows they often depend more on word order than on phonics to figure out the meaning of unfamiliar words. One problem with the Phonics approach is the complexity of the English language. The same letter or letter combination does not always represent the same sound.

Sing-songs

Rhyme is a prominent feature of many songs. Listening to and singing songs helps make children aware of the phonemic nature of spoken language. But, songs that help children to manipulate sounds in words are most effective in having children pay attention to a language's sound structure. Manipulating sounds in words can be challenging for those children in the early stages of phonemic awareness development. Therefore, children should be given many opportunities to learn the songs before they start trying to manipulate the sounds. One way that can be done is to play tapes of such songs during transitional activities such as snack time or clean-up time in order to help children become more familiar with sound play.

Onset-rime blending

Children can be helped in thinking about words as sounds when someone is able to break the words down into smaller parts. One particular way in which a syllable can be broken down is into onset, which is everything that comes before the vowel, and rime. The latter term refers to the vowel and everything that comes after it. For instance, truck could be broken down into /tr/ and /uck/. Rhyming is blending a new onset onto an old rime. Children must have a great amount of experience recognizing rhymes before they are able to produce rhymes. Among the daily activities that help early childhood classes gain these skills are by listening to rhyming stories, reciting poetry that rhymes and singing rhyming songs.

Body-coda blending

Vowels are the loudest parts of syllables, or the peak if you will. One may always stretch the vowel and say it out loud. Children can with relative ease, break syllables on either side of the loud vowel.

For example, they might break ship into sh-ip or shi-p. In discussing the body of a syllable, the reference is to all of the phonemes within the vowel. Those consonants that are found after the vowel are called codas. For instance, in the word dream, /dre/ is the body of the syllable and the coda is /m/. The reward for body-coda blending is that it is easier than onset-rime blending. The reason is because of the distortion that frequently occurs during blending.

Orthographic analogies

Orthographic analogies are word families that can be generated from knowing onsets and rimes. Using orthographic analogies help students rapidly build their reading and writing vocabularies. For instance, if a child knows the word "man," they could use a rime analogy to read or write any word that rhymes such as "tan," "fan," "can," etc. There have been studies that question the effectiveness of using orthographic analogies for young children. These studies indicate that children do not see the orthographic similarities but rather hear a word from an adult that functions as a clue rather than see the printed word that causes them to say a word that sounds similar. The studies indicate that using analogies in teaching reading may not always be helpful if an adult is required to be there so that he or she can give the word clue to a child.

Sound analysis training

Children can understand the letters in words that are printed represent the sounds in words that are spoken. Children can change single consonants at the start or end of one-syllable words upon a teacher's request, such as change "cat" to "rat." Sound analysis alone has been found to be effective in development of alphabetic principle skills. But sound analysis taught along with the relationships between sounds and letters that give practice in using these letter-sound relationships in reading and writing provides the greatest benefit. Alphabetic mapping is also useful. When children know sounds of four or five consonants they can start to develop and understanding how the alphabetic principle works. Using movable letters to showing switched letters can help show different sound combinations.

Word families

Knowing that words contain the same sound pattern will often share spelling patterns is important for a child to know. When children learn that a number of frequently occurring patterns of spelling occur and has learned that these spelling patterns can be generalized, the child will be more able to analyze and identify words with efficiency which are not recognized immediately. The major value of word families, also known as phonograms, in kindergarten is that they give the student the opportunity to practice decoding the beginning letters in a word. It should not be expected that the children will learn to use the word families in generative ways. In other words, they are not expected to learn word families as a unit with which they can decode as a means of independently decoding new words. Word families give children more practice with the application of the alphabetic principle.

Prior knowledge

Prior knowledge is information that is already known that is brought to the awareness level in order for the reader to connect new information with the known. This allows students categories on which to hang their newly acquired knowledge. Research has found that what readers bring to a text is one of the best ways to predict how they will comprehend the text. When a student uses prior knowledge, he or she has the ability to better focus on what is most important in the text. This also leads to inferences and elaboration as the text is read. Student may fill in the blanks if needed and store such information in memory by using this prior knowledge. Research has also shown that the use of predication to activate prior knowledge indicated students were more interested in what they were reading and remembered it better.

Accretion is one form of increasing prior knowledge. Each time something new is taught or referred to in a class, there are traces of it that are left in a student's memory. Tuning happens when students modify and reshape information they receive until it fits their needs. Reconstruction is when students learn something that goes against what they previously thought was true. Students can build on what they already know when they can expand on terms and information they understand. Increased background information on more in-depth ideas about a topic also helps the student better understand what is being read. Students also can provide real-life experiences to help with understanding.

Schemas

Prior knowledge and experience is something common to the various stages of reading transactions. Readers build meaning before, during and after a reading transaction based upon their interest in and prior knowledge about:

- Facts that are relative to a particular topic.
- Concepts and vocabulary that is related to those concepts.
- The principles that lie underneath and generalizations.

Readers have schemas, or organized networks of prior knowledge and experiences about certain topics which foster expectation whenever they read about those topics. When students are reading, they add to or adjust their schemas and their schema influence as well as boost their comprehension of what is being read.

Contextual cues

The knowledge a reader has in how the language works is a factor in how successful that reader will comprehend a text. For example, readers may comprehend more thoroughly if they know the position of words, punctuation marks, and word relationships within sentences. This is all done through the contextual cue systems -- graphophonic, syntactic, semantic and pragmatic -- in order to make sense out of what they have read. Proficient readers are the most concerned with meaning. They use a continuous formulation of meaning in order to figure out how much attention should be paid to the text in confirming or correcting predictions, as well as in making other predictions. Middle-level students must continue to balance the use of interacting language cuing systems in order to extract meaning from texts.

Metacognition

In the simplest terms, metacognition is the process of thinking about thinking. The concept is most often associated with John Flavell, a developmental psychologist at Stanford University. As applied to reading and writing, students can use metacognition to develop specific plans of action to enable a better understanding of the material. The three key elements of this process are: 1) designing the plan of action; 2) monitoring it; and 3) assessing its effectiveness. The process can be facilitated by encouraging students to ask a series of questions. For instance, when developing the plan, a student should ask questions such as "Why am I reading this?" and "How much time do I have?" Questions for the monitoring phase include "What information is most important?" and "What should I do if I don't understand?" Finally, the assessment phase prompts questions such as "How did I do?" and "What could I have done differently?"

Various uses of language

African-American behavior of "acting white"

Dr. John Ogbu has argued for years that the blacks have developed an oppositional cultural identity because of discrimination developed by their own culture. This stems in part from the times when blacks were asked to have the same behavior and speech as whites such as after emancipation. With the Black Power Movement of the 1960s, an oppositional cultural identity was in place where racial pride was expressed. Still, Ogbu believed that blacks still try to enter white culture. A resulting behavior derided by some, especially younger blacks, called "acting white" can be stressful for blacks. They get accused of being an Uncle Tom or disloyal to the black community. Speaking is one way in particular that blacks are labeled as talking white.

Dialect

Dialect is a regionally or socially distinctive variety of language that is characterized by particular accents, sets of words and grammar. Even though it is easy to distinguish between a dialect and a language the difference often turns out to be a matter of degree. People are said to speak different languages when they do not understand what they other is saying. They are said to speak dialects if they can understand each other, even though not perfectly. There are exceptions. A single dialect spoken usually by a majority of people and that comes to predominate as the official standard form of the language is one exception. It is also the written form of that language. Hence, the English dialect spoken by a majority of the people becomes standard English, not that it has singular linguistic features but because most people speak it that way.

Language development and reading acquisition

Social class and family background

The social class and family background variables are prominent in emergent literacy research. Numerous studies have addressed links between parental occupation, income, and children's achievements. One finding is that there are wide variations in children's achievement regardless of social class in relation to a child's early literacy experiences. Specific factors in family environments where there is parental interest, positive attitudes and modeling have all been identified as major predictors of schools success despite social class or educational levels. There is a wide variety in family environments in the status and value given to books, the presence of materials for writing and time that are spent reading and writing. Studies have shown that early readers tended to come from homes with more pencils, paper and books and have mothers who read more than often.

Parental education and socioeconomic status

The exact nature of the impact parental education and social economic status has on student achievement although it does have an impact. Studies have found that parental education and family socioeconomic status alone are not necessarily predictors of how students will achieve academically. Studies have found that parental education accounts for about a quarter of the variance in student test scores while socioeconomic status accounts for slightly more than a quarter. Other research indicates that dysfunctional home environments, low expectations from parents, parenting that is ineffective, differences in language and high mobility levels may account for the low achievement levels among those students that come from lower socioeconomic levels.

Reading proficiency importance

There is strong evidence that young people who are not fluent readers and writers by the end of the third grade may never catch up with their peers. One study found that first graders who were not on grade level by the end of the year stood a 1-in-10 chance of ever having proficiency at grade level in reading. A governor of Indiana indicated that the determination of how many new prison beds to build was based, in part, on the number of second graders who do not read at second grade level. The number of future prison beds in California depends on numbers of children who do not go past the fourth grade reading level.

Sociocultural theory

Sociocultural approaches to literacy developed out of more general sociocultural theory which came from theories of Soviet psychologist L.S. Vygotsky. The three central planks of sociocultural theory have contributed to a new interpretation of literacy: The concept of genetic analysis, social learning and mediation. Genetic or developmental analysis suggests it is possible to understand mental functional aspects by understanding their origin and transitions. From genetic analysis it is understood the futility of seeing literacy as something that is isolated. Rather, a proper understanding of the emergence of literacy has to take into account the broad cultural, social and historic factors that relate to the significance of reading and writing for human communication and cognition.

Social learning refers to the social origin of mental functioning. Vygotsky said that every function in the child's cultural development appears on the social level and later on the individual level. The first development is between people and the second is inside the child. Vygotsky also believed the development occurred through such means as apprenticeship learning, or interaction with teachers and peers. This view looks at learning not as an isolated act of cognition but rather a process of gaining entry to a discourse of practitioners. Mediation is the notion that all human activity is mediated through signs or tools. It is not so much the tools, such as computers, or writing by themselves as it is how they transform human action in a fundamental way.

Discourse theory

Discourse theory includes the view that language is either an abstract system of linguistic forms or an individual form of activity, that language is a continuous generative process that is used in a social and verbal interaction of speakers. Such views espouse more focused and increased interaction leading to higher forms of learning. It is an intense social interaction where creative energies are found through the partial or total restructuring of ideological systems. Such interactions are seen by some as most beneficial when crossing cultural boundaries. Other discourse theorists posited that it is not isolated words that learners assimilate through dialogic interaction but rather discourses and genres.

Constructivist theory

A major portion of constructivist theory is that learning is an active process in which those who learn build new ideas or concepts based upon their current and/or past knowledge. Those who learn select and transform information, build a hypothesis and makes decisions that rely on a cognitive structure in order to make it work. Cognitive structures such as mental models or schema provide meaning and organization to experiences. This lets the individual go beyond the information that is given there. In constructivist theory, instruction should address:

- A predisposition towards learning.
- The different ways knowledge can be built so that the learner most readily grasps it.
- The most effective sequences in which material can be presented.
- The nature as well as pacing of rewards and punishments.

Social constructivism

Social constructivism is a variant of cognitive constructivism that shows and emphasis on the collaborative nature of learning. This theory was developed by Soviet psychologist Lev Vygotsky. He was a cognitivist but he rejected postulations by other cognitivists such as Piaget and Perry that separating learning from its social context was possible. Vygotsky theorized that all cognitive functions originate and must be explained as products of social interactions and that learning was not simply the accommodation and assimilation of new knowledge attained by those learning. Instead, he felt it was the process by which learners were integrated into a community of knowledge. Vygotsky believed that the cultural development of children appear, first on the social level and secondly inside the child. This applies in voluntary attention to logical memories and forming concepts, all equally. Higher functions come from actual relationships between people, Vygotsky postulated.

Cultural constructivism

Cultural constructivism is a theory asserting that knowledge and reality are products of their cultural context. This means that two independent cultures will likely form different methodologies of observation. Western cultures usually utilize objects for making scientific descriptions, while Native American culture uses events to describe phenomena. Beyond social environments for learning are wider cultural influences such as custom, language, religion, biology and tools. The tools such as language and symbols that people use can have an effect on the way they think, according to this theory. There are some schools of thought that tools redistribute the cognitive load of some task between people and the tool while they are used. For instance, a telephone can change a conversation's nature.

Sapir-Whorf hypothesis

The Sapir-Whorf hypothesis says that a systematic relationship exists between grammatical categories of the language a person speaks and how the person thinks and behaves in it. The hypothesis was actually an axiom developed by anthropologist Edward Sapir and his student and colleague Benjamin Whorf. The hypothesis is also known as the principle of linguistic relativity. There are arguments to the version of this idea that thought is constrained by language. One argument is that all people have problems occasionally expressing themselves due to language and known the language is inadequate for what they are meaning to say. Thus, thought is not a set of words because a concept can be understood without it being expressed with words. Arguments also exist for the extreme opposite, that language does not at all influence thought.

Socratic questioning

Socratic questioning is at the heart of critical thinking skills. It is more than just having a one-word answer or an agreement and disagreement from students. Socratic questions make students make assumptions, sort through points that are relevant and irrelevant as well as explain those points. This instruction can take many different forms including:
- Raising basic issues.
- Probing beneath the surface of matters.
- Pursing areas of thought fraught with problems.
- Helping students find the structure of their own thinking.
- Helping students develop clarity, accuracy and relevance.
- Helping students make judgments by reasoning on their own.
- It also helps students think about evidence, conclusions, assumptions, implications, points of view, concepts and interpretations.

The following are question categories that make Socratic questioning usable by teachers:
- Clarifying questions. These questions that ask for more information, verification, clarifying a main idea or point, students building on an opinion, explaining a certain statement or rephrasing content.
- Assumption-probing questions. These questions ask for verification, explanation, reliability or clarification.
- Probing evidence and reasons. Such questions ask for more examples, reasons for statements, evidence, asking if reasons are adequate, asking how the process led to the belief and anything that

might cause a change in the student's point of view.

- Questions about perspectives and points of view. These questions look for a particular viewpoint's alternatives, how others might respond, or compare differences and similarities among points of view.
- Questions probing consequences and implications. These questions describe implications of what is said, the cause and effect of actions and alternatives.
- Questions about questions. These break the question into smaller questions or concepts for added evaluation.

Critical questioning and critical thinking

Critical thinking requires a systematic monitoring of thought. Critical thought must not be accepted at face value but should be analyzed for accuracy, clarity, breadth, logicalness, and depths. Critical thinking also requires that reasoning occur within various points of views and frames of reference and that all reasoning stems from goals and objectives and has an informational base. When data are used for reasoning it must be interpreted and the interpretation involves concepts that contain assumptions and that all inferences in thought have implication. The result of critical thought is that the basic questions of Socrates can be framed more focally and used, leading to question:

- Ends and objectives.
- Wording of questions.
- Sources of information and fact.
- Method and quality of information collected.
- Assumptions that are behind the concepts being used.

Integrated nature of the English language arts

Reading-writing connection

Reading and writing are generally viewed as two sides of the same coin. Reading leads to writing and vice-versa. When a child reads, he learns structure, punctuation and vocabulary, all of which can make him a better writer and a better reader. To help make the connection, a teacher may require a student to keep a journal in which he writes about what he reads. The process of writing will help the student analyze and question what he has read. Therefore, a journal can also be a vital tool for enhancing metacognition. For older students, a classroom debate would require students to read pertinent material and then write position papers. Another metacognitive approach to making the reading-writing connection is the KWL chart. Before reading new material, students will be asked to write down what they Know about the topic and what they Want to know. Afterwards, they will write down what they Learned.

Reading, writing and speaking

Language is developed as it is being used and in response to the demands that are made on it in different content areas as well as in life experiences. A number of factors shape language including the nature of the speaker or writer and the audience, the relationship between the two, the purpose of speaking and writing, the nature of the subject and the medium that is used. A wide variety of tasks in which language is used enhances language development. Students acquire most of their learning through language. The development of language is also enhanced by the various opportunities to use language in many different situations to attend to varied tasks.

Writing and speaking

Distinctions between writing and speech are fundamental to discussions that surround language. The movement of phonic substance through the vocal organs is the transmitting mechanism for speech, while graphic substance in which marks are made on a surface by a hand are the transportation modes of writing. Other aspects of relationship between writing and speech are less physical. Both writing and speech occur in situations in which there is communication. Differences also are found in the language structure between the two. The contrasts that are found in writing also do not correspond to those that can be used within a system of sound. For instance, it may be difficult to pronounce contrasts between words that look and sound alike but have different meanings.

Effects of various factors on literacy

Relationship between home and school literacy

Studies have shown that a positive relation exists between children's literacy experiences at home and how easy it is for the child to transition to school. Family literacy environments do differ in some aspects. The development of print awareness appears to be common across cultures, major differences occur in the quantity of exposure children have had with the written language and reading storybooks in particular. There also is a difference in the perceptions of the roles parents have in their children's literacy experiences. Studies have found such family characteristics relating to reading achievement includes parental aspirations for the child, academic guidance, attitude toward education and having reading materials in the home.

Storybook reading at home is a key component in early literacy acquisition, according to several studies. Studies have documented the relationship between reading to children and their later success on reading readiness tasks. It has been found that children who are read to can easily acquire concepts about the function of written language in books. Findings show that most successful early readers have had contact at home with written material. When poor readers enter school they have had much less experience with books and reading than those who become better at reading. In short, children learn how to attend to language and apply that knowledge to literacy situations by interacting with others who model functions of language.

School readiness is influenced by their parents' educational levels. The higher the parents' education the more likely the child will succeed in school. Children who are raised in literate homes are likely to enter first grade with several thousand hours of 1-to-1 pre-reading experience. Children have a better chance of becoming fully literate adults if they are encouraged to read at home. Studies have shown that improving parents' skills positively affects the children's language development. Without parental support, the cycle of under-education will continue in families from generation to generation. With support from family literacy programs, children who may have been educationally and developmentally behind their peers came into school on par with their peers.

Places to learn literacy

Literacy does not just come from going to school. It is learned everywhere including the reading of bus stop signs and boxes of cereal to listening to family stories in the language of the home and on the Internet. Caregivers as well as parents have a profound impact of their children's readiness upon entering school. The influence grows and changes each year. The positive influence of the family continues in importance as the children develop through elementary, junior high and high school. It can be helped by meaningful involvement by engaging parents, having parents and children participate in literacy activities together and helping adults help children with adult education. Likewise, peers and community members will all play a significant part as well in developing literacy among each other.

Peer influence

Peer influence on children's behavior as well as on literacy development is well recognized in psychological literature. Peer influence can operate both ways, positive and negative. Teachers will try normally to exploit the positive influence on peers and promote many of the learning experiences the children may have by organizing them into small groups in which they can become involved in learning. The negative aspects of peer influence are obvious when parents of children expect him and her to show interest in school work and spend time on homework but many of the children's peers do not have the same goals on their agendas. It is under such circumstances that it might become necessary to have the child discontinue his or her association with those peers who are negative influences.

Students, teenagers specifically, look to each other to learn and this sometimes brings about problems. Teenagers are growing and learning and through this development the students look toward each other to acquire what their peers deem to be acceptable. In many instances this may lead to inaccurate understandings. Teenagers purposely acquire knowledge sometimes that is unmistakably wrong and continue to use

it in everyday situations. Some students are so influenced by their culture that, even though they are capable of speaking properly, they will not do so for fear they will not fit in with their peers. These students who have been properly taught will acknowledge to adults that they are speaking in slang, yet they continue to speak slang because their culture has shaped them to do so.

Dissonance and congruence

Student success appears to be related to congruence between home and school socialization. Studies show that high achievers have a home environment that is congruent with a school environment. High achievers learned how to independently and obediently complete tasks at home. Such behaviors are important to school success as well. A dissonance between home and school may be caused by cultural differences in some cases. Some studies have indicated black children prefer and do better in communal learning settings while white students like and do better in those settings that are competitive. Cultural dissonance may also lead to wrong interpretations of parent behaviors that create misunderstandings between school and home.

Predictions of student academic achievement can be made from looking at the congruence between the home and school cultures of children. Students have the tendency to be more successful when both their home and school cultures have similarities. There also tends to be less success when a disconnection is there between the home and the school cultures. Moving from the familiar environment of the home to a more unfamiliar environment at the school can especially result in disconnection for many minority and low-income students. This can be minimized or eliminated when the schools work with the students and their families in helping both adapt to the school environment.

Parental expectations

Research has found that parental expectations are significant to school performance as well as critical to achievement in academics. The high expectations from parents are usually found in association with levels of educational attainment that are higher. Parenting practices that are effective and associated with high levels of academic achievement include expectations that children receive high numerical grades of their schoolwork. Additionally, research indicates that child rearing beliefs, ways to academically enrich home environments and standards of behavior that are acceptable both in and out of school are likewise important to achieving academically. Insofar as behavior is concerned, the children who succeed have the adaptability to conforming to behavioral standards at school, something many have already learned through parental expectations.

Community and family partnerships

Literacy programs that involve parent and community components can be created in a number of ways. Some will focus on the school aspect, others on the parents or community as the most active part of the program. Both approaches have the same goal, which is a literacy program that engages all the members of a community in ensuring children are literate. A formal school, family and community partnership is one way to meet such goals. This is a comprehensive program that consists of activities that are chosen by each school to help students reach goals in literacy. Partnerships that are well-organized can create goal-oriented activities that help student reach high levels of achievement in literacy.

Most everyone in education agrees that parents and local communities should be involved in education. Studies show children do better when parents are involved in their children's schools. Community members can become involved in schools, acting as role models and mentors and giving an extra measure of support for both students and teachers. There is no one approach for getting schools, parents and communities together for literacy programs. But there are different types of activities that will help parents, schools and communities work together in support literacy. This includes assistance with parenting, communicating, volunteering, reading at home, decision-making and collaborating with the community. Programs that are design need to consider a community's unique character and its needs in starting a community and family involvement program.

Literature written for students

Mediating children's literature

The model of mediation is a general and dynamic framework that is meat to guide problem solving for teachers. It does not serve as a guide to analyze discriminate tasks or a list of what is the next step. It is dynamic because it both evolves and guides through the social interaction that takes place in learning. When the teacher is interacting with a student, he or she continually analyzes how the student thinks and what strategies they use in problem solving. The analysis tells the teacher what type of support to provide and how much should be given. The goal of instructional mediation is to help learners develop their own self-directed system of mediation, to become self-directed and independent readers. The decision-making process for the teacher looks at the purpose, the strategies and the reflection.

High interest, low vocabulary books

Books that have a high interest and low vocabulary are materials with controlled vocabularies and reading difficulty levels. But the material also has plot and topics that are appropriate to the older students. It gives an older student, such as a young teen, the opportunity to read without having to read something that might be embarrassing for the teen because it is intended for much smaller children. These high interest and low vocabulary books must also provide supports for those with reading problems just as the early picture books. This includes illustrations that support text, vocabulary that is carefully chosen, an appropriate vocabulary load, simple sentences, characters that interest readers and compelling stories.

Multicultural literature

There are a number of considerations in selecting multicultural literature for children. They include:

- Accuracy. Books should have current and accurate information. Stories should acknowledge events that are recent.
- Stereotypes. Books should reflect the lives of individual people rather than giving general behaviors or personality traits to an entire group of people.
- Setting. The settings in books should be accurate and, again, avoiding stereotypes.
- Language. Be careful in selecting books that might separate characters into groups of those who speak standard English and those who do not.
- Epithets. Some books may contain racial or ethnic epithets.

- Illustrations. The illustrations should show that those in ethnic groups look different from one another.

Adolescent literature

A number of reasons exist why adolescent literature is important. The reasons include:
- It helps adolescents understand various concerns and issues.
- It is a safe place to read real-world experiences. Reading in a medium that is open-ended and not threatening allows students to empathize with others, as well as to consider and understand a wide variety of circumstances and the consequences of what takes place.
- It helps students discover their place in the world in unique and helps them to discover themselves.
- It provides models that assist them in dealing with the problems that they may face every day. Adolescents with troubles may identify with the characters and act as a way to help them in solving the problems that they have.

Literary genres

Text structure of different genres

A reader's knowledge about the text patterns and structures of different genres and their ability to use those understandings about structure and elements effectively all help to formulate meaning. For example, poems may rhyme or have repeating patterns, expository passages develop logically, short stories or novels have elements such as characters and setting, headings indicate the major text sections and summaries sum up the main points of a text. When students become aware of the text structure, they will better understand what is being read and will remember it for longer periods. Readers use text knowledge to tell the difference between narrative and expository reading and will accordingly adapt their reading strategies.

Comic books

Children have been reading comic books since before the middle of the 20th century. Researchers investigated using comic books in stimulating students in language arts classes because of their popularity. One pair of researchers, Wright and Sherman, suggested that teachers should use comic strips in language arts classes for three reasons:

- Their student showed a high level of interest in the particular genre.
- The wide circulation of comic strips makes them a very viable source of material economically.
- Most comic strips have readability levels that are low, with words and sentences that are linguistically apt for readers of elementary and middle school levels.

Comics, TV, drama and other multimedia formats may provide a way to reach even more language arts students and keeping them engaged in the study of literacy skills.

Media literacy

Media literacy includes both reading (decoding) and writing (encoding) media messages. It is a communication that is a basic for the traditional idea of literacy. The skills or competencies involved in media literacy also enter many content areas and are able to be integrated across the curriculum in the same manner that writing and reading are required skills beyond language arts and English curriculum. Some state educational curricula have begun to incorporate media literacy, requiring students in some states to understand the selection of all media in news coverage, draw conclusions about the media's reports and the public's response as well as recognize propaganda. While some misuses of television and videotape has taken place in some classrooms there is a much better recognition of the value of media literacy.

Multimedia literacy
Multimedia literacy is an aspect of literacy that is being recognized as technology expands how people communicate with each other. Literacy, as a concept, emerged as a measure of how one can read or write. It means today that someone reads or writes at a level that is adequate to communicate. Multimedia calls for a more fundamental meaning of literacy when looked upon at a societal level. Multimedia is the use of several different media to send or receive information. These include text, audio, graphics, animation, virtual reality, computer programming and robotics. Basic literacy of reading and writing are often done by computer these days and provides a foundation for more advanced levels of multimedia literacy.

Film and television
Television and video can help explore cultural context and are easily integrated into the curriculum. They are entertaining media and allow for a great deal of flexibility in techniques of teaching and material. Surveys indicate that more teachers than ever are integrating television and videotapes into the curricula. Teachers are seeking quality programming with the appropriate structure and length as well as advance information that allows them to preview the programming. Also found in the

surveys was that both teachers and students are becoming more media savvy and use with increased frequency camcorders and other video production equipment. That is likely to grow even more with such mobile video platforms as digital cameras and cell phones.

Television news and documentaries have long been used in secondary and postsecondary classrooms for writing instruction. There have been suggestions that the structure and content of news presentations mirror the writing of essays and can help in serving in effecting writing instruction. A selected TV program can be perused in one class period with students asking questions and giving comments. Student can also produce outlines for the news report and the outlines are collected at the end of the class period. Advertising images, magazines and television series may also help promote critical thinking during the writing process.

Trade books

Trade books are written specifically for students but are not textbooks. They may be used to help improve reading skills, develop knowledge of content areas and to further understanding of the world. Trade books can be a valued complement to teaching and curriculum. They may also affect the appreciation a student has for content-related literature. These books should not replace thorough instruction in reading skills. Trade books also are not an alternative to teaching concepts of content areas. But the texts can help students understand concepts by putting them into an appropriate context. Teachers can use strategies such as this to help develop better reading skills and help students comprehend the text.

Some educators say stories about heroes serve as a source for teaching values. Some studies indicate recent trends on teaching values in connection with methods of analysis. Personal models such as heroes in history, fiction and current events all help to exemplify and encourage emulation of certain virtues or desirable traits of character such as civility, courage, honesty, perseverance, self-restraint, compassion, fairness as well as respect for the dignity of individuals and being responsible for the common good. Trade books are a good source for using heroes to teach values. These stories should be accurate and present both positive and negative aspect of a person's life. Multimedia instruction, including the use of videotapes, can help add depth to the portrayal.

Language arts can be infused into content areas such as mathematics and science by using trade books. This includes picture books, fiction, and nonfiction books that are other than text books. Trade books, according to studies, appeal to a student's imagination and curiosity even more than text books. They also help students understand concepts by showing them in language that is familiar. Literature can help students make personal connections to ideas in math and science by putting these subjects into contexts that are meaningful and familiar. Some of these trade books may not be specifically about math or science but perhaps show characters who relate activities about math and science. Such strategies help students gain confidence in such subjects and develop perseverance in solving problems.

Electronic textbooks

Technology is commonly used for learning such as elementary science students watching a videodisc of an experiment being performed, middle school students manipulating commercial software that helps them prepare for a rapidly-changing, technological workplace, and high school students playing interactive chemistry games on the Internet that score their manipulations of chemical equations and formulas to solve problem in real life. Technology can help a child who is blind to hear audible descriptions that allow him or her to understand procedures and participate in a particular portion of class. Students who are physically impaired can complete computer activities with commercial software that has adaptive devices to permit the student to independently complete a task. Students who are hearing impaired can use CD-ROM or Internet video with captions.

Application of Theoretical & Knowledge Bases of Reading in Instruction

Literate environment

Role of newspapers

Students learn when they are motivated in the topics they study have interest and relevance to their lives. Many classrooms are using newspapers as a source for some very good motivational and timely resources. It is a concept that dates back to 1795 when the Portland Eastern Herald in Maine published an editorial that put forth the role that newspapers can play in helping to deliver, extend and enrich the curriculum. Classrooms around the world are using newspapers to compliment text books and other relevant resources for a variety of disciplines. Newspaper feature articles, editorial and advertising help students apply literacy and numeracy skills as well as to appreciate the importance of studying history and current affairs. Studies have shown that students who use newspapers score higher on reading comprehension tests and develop stronger critical thinking skills.

Four-way sharing group

A group using a four-way share can be used for any content area and gets students to listen to and generate oral language. The four-way sharing helps provide equal access to all students and helps to manage the talk in the classroom, especially after a charged issue. Four students sit on the floor facing each other from the positions of the cardinal directions. The teacher directs the "North" to speak for a full five minutes and the rest of the group will listen. Each of the other directions get five minutes. It might be helpful to start with a much shorter time period until the students are comfortable doing the circuits. Teachers can find out how effective students use speaking and listening time in this strategy as well.

Computer use

Laptop computers, the programs that bring laptops to students for their use and various network connections, students may use laptops in the classroom, take them on field trips or go home with the students. If they are used appropriately, laptops can help develop project-based learning and multimedia activities as students work to collect data, brainstorm or produce projects. Among the advantages:

- They are portable within the school and outside of class.
- They may be taken on field trips and used for investigations.
- They can provide immediate data processing and graphic feedback.
- Feedback and analysis that is immediate prompts next-step decision-making in the field.
- It allows files to be shared.
- The computers generate reports and projects.
- They can provide access to experts through e-mail or the Internet.

There is a potential for students to engage in behavior with computers that is not intended, such as "surfing the 'net." Many schools have written guidelines for the use of computers in school as well as have teachers sign statements that acknowledge they know the rules for using the computers. Teachers should adopt management schemes that are meant to limit problems and make sure computers are used appropriately. These are some possible considerations that teachers may opt for when using computers in class:

- There is zero tolerance for misusing laptops.
- A "lids down" or "think time" should be designated to ensure the students attention is directed at the teacher.
- Planning should be done ahead for recharging batteries.
- Identical software programs should be installed.
- Software shortcuts should be set up.
- Students should save files in specific directories.

It can be a challenge to have multimedia activities with only one computer in class but it can be done using strategies to get the most student access. The computer can accordingly be used a presentation platform for both teacher and student, such as through the use of Power Point-style programs. A single computer may also function as a learning or research center or as a small-group development station. A projection unit or TV converter can be used to make the computer as a presentation platform. The teacher can demonstrate, provide and use teaching techniques that are technologically-enhanced. Students can also show their projects to the class. As a learning or research center, computers can be set up where students can find multimedia encyclopedias, the Internet and various application software such as word processors.

A classroom with several computers can be used for a combination of platforms including as presentation tools, learning centers, development stations or a combination of those configurations. A classroom with several computers will

have computers available when many of the students need them. Students also can leave projects that are in the works on the classroom computer and known that their work would not be disturbed by other classes. Having several classroom computers give the opportunity for more flexibility in class than in having to use a computer lab but it also has less flexibility than having laptops available for all the students. Research has found that at least three computers in a classroom are necessary to ensure that each student can get some time during a class period on the computer.

A classroom which is equipped with computers for all students might resemble a computer lab to some students so teachers should make attendance rules well known to get the class off to a better beginning. A routine also may need to be established for students who are put off by the non-traditional roles that computer technology has them assume. Pacing is also a concern in a classroom with computers. Fewer activities exist for students to work on at their own pace than those that are carefully-timed activities during class periods. Teachers who set goals and activities for a class at the beginning of a class and then let students work at their own pace usually are more comfortable with computers in the classroom.

Technology

Various lessons can be enriched by the use of technology. This includes:

- Digital presentations. Students can show their learning in a digital presentation. They might create a Web site or create a stand-alone presentation. Students should cite their sources of information as with any research project. They should also be taught the importance of seeking permission for copyrighted matter.

- Have students read books online. Thousands of books are available online at Web sites such as Online Books Page.
- Have Web quests. This is an activity that is good for language arts and exploration of literature. The quest list sets of questions and task on which students can perform Internet research.
- Word processing. Word processing programs are good for projects that would require having multiple drafts.

Technology can be used in lessons for a host of content areas. Some examples include:

- Language arts. The Internet can be used to look at photos described in novels and can provide information about the social fabric of the community, helping the student learn the context.
- Mathematics. Spreadsheets can be used to figure out distance, speed and weather conditions as well as the travel time between two cities. The data can be exposed in several forms to help foster the understanding of variables.
- Science. Look at topographic and satellite maps to help determine an area's rock formations.
- Physical education. Look at basketball techniques in slow motion to help improve shooting.

Children who are young can benefit from using technology. Technology can be a resource for teachers, students and parent. Research has shown that students using technology have higher achievement levels and enhance their basic skills in reading, writing and math if they can practice those skills with the use of technology. Students are engaged for longer time periods with the use of technology. It intensifies their basic tasks in learning. Technology can motivate students to learn which help increases their desire to go to school and continue on to college. It can give students a chance to explore other lands through the Internet. Instruction can be enhanced by the use of visual aids and lessons on the Internet to boost comprehension.

Book clubs

Student-organized and student-driven book clubs help to build a community in the classroom and to encourage students to read independently. They are in effect taking responsibility for their learning of literacy. Book clubs let students choose what they want to read, where they read, how they read it and with whom they read. The choice is valued by students. Students must work together to negotiate places and times to meet, along with the pacing and discussion of their books in order to have successful book clubs. They learn valuing one another as readers and learners. Teachers can allow book clubs to meet a small-group times during reading in order to give the students freedom in operating their own club.

Activities in which groups can build for book clubs at school include:

- Letting the group name themselves. Let them decide on a club mascot.
- Allow each club to keep a group reading notebook or journal where they track their readings. Perhaps they might decorate the journal if they so wish.
- Groups may decide upon projects that are inquiry-based. For example, a group might decide to explore something of specific interest to them and search for

the information. After these steps are taken, teachers should explain the process and allow some class time so that students may discuss the activities and establish their first groups. Those students who are not interested in this voluntary activity can read on their own.

Promoting literacy as a lifelong skill

Lifelong learning is important in the lives of people in general and specifically, teachers. The rapid changes in the social, technological and economic world have made people prepare for a second or even third career and to keep themselves up on new developments that impact their goals personally and socially. Lifelong learners keep their senses active and think of new ideas. Much of the learning is self-directed. Skill for lifelong learning include the ability to ask questions, form hypotheses, use the right resources to answer questions, read with comprehension, and to take in information and evaluate it. Preparing students to be lifelong learners will require the skills to continually seek knowledge.

Reading comprehension strategies

Fluency

Fluency is key to becoming competent as a reader. It involves getting words right as well as phrasing and proper intonation. Children who are younger readers engage in stop and start reading. These children are spending most of their time decoding text. But studies have shown that the more time children give to text decoding, the less they will comprehend the text. Studies also show that higher-order skills such as synthesizing, analyzing and

summarizing require fluency in reading. A lack of comprehension in reading affects all content areas. Because student cannot read fluently, their time is spent decoding the words rather than taking in the text from which they should be learning.

The amount of practice that is required for fluency and automaticity in reading by children varies. Some children can read a word once and then recall it again with more speed. Other youngsters may need exposures numbering 20 or more. On average, children need between four and 14 exposures to have automaticity in the recognition of new words. Thus, it is vital that children who are learning reading read a large amount of text at their independent reading level and that the format of the text provides practice that is specific for the skills being learned. Fluency and automaticity in reading words -- along with phonemic awareness and phonics skills -- are necessary but not sufficient in constructing meaning from text. They must understand what is being read.

Fluency and reading comprehension are closely related. By learning to read accurately, children are able to comprehend text. Also, research shows that students who score low on fluency tests also tend to score low on reading comprehension assessments. Fluency is not the same as automaticity which refers to a reader's ability to recognize words automatically, accurately and rapidly. Fluency involves reading connected passages with little effort and with expression. Automatic word recognition is important, but is insufficient as a skill for developing fluency. Fluent readers are able to read grade-level text with 90 percent accuracy and a rate of about 90 words per minute. They are also able to demonstrate comprehension of text when they read aloud.

Developing fluency requires extensive practice and exposure to reading. Research indicates that repeated oral reading is particularly effective for readers who are both beginning and struggling. This practice can help improve accuracy, word recognition, speed and fluency. It may also lead to an increased reading comprehension. Students benefit from reading the same story aloud several times until they are fluent enough to read the passage independently. This sometimes takes three or four times but how often it is repeated varies depending on the student. Practicing by reading aloud sight words from lists is not sufficient in improving fluency. This is because the student may be able to recognize a sight word in isolation but still be unable to read it.

Study strategies

Two-column note taking

Two-column note taking will find a student drawing a lengthwise line down the middle of a piece of paper. As the student reads or listens, the major concepts or headings are noted in the left-hand space and the supporting details are recorded in the right column. Only one side of the paper is used. When it is time to study, the paper is folded down the center so that either the main ideas or the details can be seen, but both cannot be seen. This helps a student studying for an essay test recall details while looking at main ideas. For multiple choice tests, the student tries to recall main ideas while looking at the details. The notes are a memory device that is more efficient than either recalling from memory or rereading.

Note-taking challenges

Reading for certain information and then taking notes are perhaps the most challenging step in the process of solving information problems. Students in grades 3-8 require many developmentally-appropriate chances to locate information before the techniques are mastered. Note-taking consists of identifying keywords and related words, skimming and scanning, and extracting needed information. These steps start after students define and narrow the task as well as construct researchable questions then find the right sources. After students build researchable questions from the information needed to finish a task or solve an information problem, the questions can be transferred to graphic organizers or data charts. This can allow them to focus on the key words. Skimming and scanning will help them use text with less time and effort. Information may be extracted and recorded with different forms of note-taking including citation, summary, quotation and paraphrasing.

Test-taking strategies

A reason for test anxiety and poor performance on tests is often a lack of preparation. Children will often know about a test in advance. Some teachers also tell parents when tests will be given. Knowing when the test will be and what is to be covered can help give the child a study schedule to prepare for the test. One schedule is for the student to study nightly, for several nights before the test. Teachers may encourage parents to determine how long the child can be expected to concentrate at a given sitting. The parent should also be encouraged by the teacher to ask the child what material might be on the test and go over questions at the end of chapters and sections. Maps, charts and diagrams should receive special attention. A sample test can be developed from this information which can even make studying fun.

Before a test students should:
- Begin to study the material a few days before the test and take study breaks every 20-30 minutes.
- Take time to do some kind of physical activity that will help reduce tension and stress.
- Eat a good breakfast the morning of the test and get a good night's sleep during the night before the test.
- Skim the material and determine which parts are best understood and which ones are still difficult.
- Read a sentence or two and reread what you don't understand.
- Pick out main ideas or key terms. Think up by yourself possible test questions.
- Read aloud and study with a partner or parent. While reading the student should listen to himself.
- Think about what important points the teacher talked about during class.
- Remain motivated and positive.

There are particular test-taking strategies appropriate for elementary students. Students should follow directions carefully. Have the student listen and read the directions to the test so they understand what is expected of them. Teachers need to make sure the students understand vocabulary words and concepts in the directions. Words appearing in the test directions that are common should be introduced to students as part of the process of test preparation. Ensure the students understand what they are to do. If they have questions they should be encouraged to ask the teacher before the test starts. Listening and reading activities can be incorporated into the classroom that will provide practice for following directions. Students need to know how to budget their time for the test. They should work fast but comfortably. Students can practice this.

Multiliteracies

A great deal of interest has risen around the world in the future of literacy teaching through so-called "multiliteracies." The multiliteracies argument is that our personal, public and working lives are changing these days in some very significant ways and these changes have the effect of transforming cultures and the way we communicate. The ramification of this is that the way literacy is now taught is obsolete and what counts for literacy must also change. There are two major and closely related changes associated with multiliteracies. First is the growing significance of cultural and linguistic diversity. This is reinforced every day by modern media. We must negotiate the differences each day in our local communities as well as at work. As this happens, English is becoming a world language. The second major shift is the influence of new communications technologies.

Ausubel's theory of meaningful learning

The major idea in Ausubel's theory is the hierarchical organization of knowledge and that new information is meaningful in that it can be related to that which is already known. The theory stresses this type of learning rather than rote learning or memorization as well as received knowledge instead of discovery learning. Ausubel postulated four processes which are environments for meaningful learning. Derivative subsumption describes a situation in which new information learned is an example of something one has already learned. Correlative subsumption is a process of accommodating new information such as a when one is used to seeing blue skies and encounters gray. Superordinate learning classifies information such as learning different types of clouds. Finally, combinatorial learning describes a process in which a new idea stems from another idea but has neither a higher nor lower hierarchy.

Reading apprenticeship model

A reading apprenticeship is a model developed from the reconceptualization of content reading. This instructional platform is centered on the dual ideas of literacy as complex social and cognitive processes and of teaching as a cognitive apprenticeship. For adolescents to move from being beginners to experts in certain content area practices, the subject matter teacher as expert practitioner guides, makes explicit, models and supports the apprentice in his or her development. Because ways of thinking, speaking, reading and writing differ from subject matter to subject matter, some see the most appropriate setting for students to learn these specific practices is from teachers who already have expertise in these fields. A reading apprenticeship involves student and teacher as partners of a collaboration that inquires into reading and reading processes as content area texts are engaged.

There are four integrated dimensions of classroom life that is explored together by student and teacher in a reading apprenticeship: social, personal, cognitive and knowledge building. The social dimension is based on constructing a community of readers using literacy as a way to connect between their interests, each other and the social world that they are learning about. The personal dimension involves building students'

awareness of themselves as readers, why they are reading and what they hope to accomplish. The cognitive dimension is part of the structure that includes instruction in and the use of strategies for comprehension, monitoring tools, and reading flexibility. Knowledge-building is centered on areas such as building schemata, or content knowledge, the vocabulary of the subject matters and structures of text and language.

Cubing

Cubing is a literacy strategy in which students are able to explore topics from six separate dimensions or viewpoints. The student can:

- Provide a description of the particular topic.
- Compare the topic to a different topic.
- Associate the topic with something else and provide specific reasons for the choice.
- Analyzing the topic and telling how the topic came about.
- Give an explanation of what the topic is composed after analysis.
- Providing an argument for or against the topic. The teacher chooses a topic related to the thematic unit. Students are divided into six groups. Students brainstorm about their dimension ideas and then use a quick write or quick draw. These are shared with the class and are attached to the sides of a cube box. This strategy can be applicable to subjects such as social studies.

History frames/story map

A history frames/story map strategy is used in helping a student think on the major points of a history story by:

- Identifying the important individuals who are a part of the story.
- Summarizing in a succinct manner the story by highlighting its main events.
- Putting the story into context and realizing the problem that was to be overcome or the goal to be achieved.
- Explaining the outcome.
- Relating the story to history, to themselves and the world.

Four graphic organizers are used, the history frame, story map, story pyramid and framed character. The history frame can be used by students who choose main events from a chapter and fill in varying sections for participants, goals, summary and resolution. The story map can be used for individual articles or for excerpts from oral histories, biographies or to help understand motives of key historical players.

Student strengths and needs

An important part of planning and organizing for instruction is to acquire an understanding of the students. It is useful, early in the school year, to learn as much as possible about the students, what their interests are, and what are their learning abilities and styles. As a teacher talks directly with each student, information is provided about how that student perceives himself or herself as a learner. Also useful is to:
- Give oral or written diagnostic questionnaires or surveys to assess the students' current abilities, interests and attitude.
- Consult other personnel, student portfolios and the students' records from previous years.
- Consider the potential for using previously successful adaptations with each student and plan other

adaptation to address the specific needs for learning.

Learning styles inventory

A teacher wants to know what types of learning styles a student has as well as other questions. These are the questions teachers must determine how instruction may be differentiated for his or her students. This also can be surprising information for the students as well. A student learning style inventory can help build self-esteem by helping the student to find out his or her strengths, learn about the areas in which more effort is required and to appreciate the differences among students. A number of published inventories are available to help students determine their learning strengths. Inventories may also be found for free on the Internet.

Grouping

Between-class ability
Between-class ability grouping is not a strategy in which all students can learn. Students at the top level seem to benefit but middle and lower students may not. It is nonetheless a popular practice in American education. The problem may lie more with the method of grouping than with the concept. Ability groups are mostly determined by standardized test or basic skills tests. But students may not have uniform knowledge and aptitude of the content areas. Another problem found in research is that teachers' expectations and the quality of instruction are often lower for lower-track groups in between-class grouping. Students may also lower their own expectations when placed in a lower-level group. This may affect self-concept in academic achievement, and thus, affect the teacher's expectations.

Within-class ability
Research tends to support within-class ability grouping, grouping those with like

abilities, as helping most students learn. It is generally flexible and not as stigmatizing as other groups. If such groups are considered then teachers might want only two such groups to help make management of the grouping process easier.

Cooperative learning
Cooperative learning is an instructional strategy in which students are put into heterogeneous groups. It is perhaps one of the best researched innovations in recent times and can have dramatic student achievement effects when implemented properly.

Individualized instruction
Individualized instruction or one-on-one instruction is the best way to deal with individual student difference but it is very difficult to accomplish. Computer-assisted instruction may change that.

Small learning groups
Small group reading instruction has been shown in a number of studies to be more effective than instruction of the class as a whole. Most of these studies did not include students who were disabled. Teacher-led groups of between three to 10 students help them learn much more than when they are taught using instruction of the whole class. Smaller groups of three to four are usually more efficient than larger groups in terms of time, peer interaction and improved skills.

Combined grouping
Combinations of formats also produce reading benefits that are measurable especially for those children with disabilities. For instance, students who work in pairs for two days in small and in small groups for two days can be combined with whole-class instruction for a part of a period.

Combined classes are those which include more than one grade level in a classroom. These classes are sometimes referred to as split classes, blended classes or double-year classes. These classes usually will include the required curriculum for each of the two grades that are represented. But some class activities may take place with children who are from both of the combined grades. This type of grouping takes place more frequently in smaller schools as well as on occasion in larger schools when the number of children in different age cohorts tend to have fluctuated. The main purpose of such classes appears to be the maximization of personnel and space resources instead of capitalizing on the diversity of ability and experience within the groups of mixed ages.

Nongraded or upgraded grouping
Nongraded and ungraded grouping usually refers to grouping children in classes without designation of grade levels and with age spans of more than one year. The original rationale was to increase the heterogeneity of class compositions and liberate children and teachers from rigid achievement expectations that are based on the age of a student. But research later found that implementing these classes tended to result in homogeneous grouping of children for children based on ability and achievement level despite age. In many instances of nongraded groups, children in classes are put in regular or temporary groups for specific instruction regardless of age. In such approaches, the main goal is to increase homogeneity of ability of groups rather than interaction across ability group lines.

Continuous progress
Continuous progress generally means that children remain with their classroom peers in an age cohort despite having met or surpassed specific grade-level achievement expectations. This term is

usually associated with the emphasis on the individualized curriculum so that teaching and learning tasks are responsive to previous experience and the rates of progress of the child despite age. This practice is sometimes referred to as social promotion. The main reason for the practice is that there might be a stigmatizing effect on children if removed from one's age cohort. The programs that are focused on continuous progress, like ungraded approaches, are not aimed at maximizing the educational benefits of children of different abilities and ages being together. Instead it is to let the children progress without being made to meet expectations of achievement.

Mixed-age or multi-age grouping

Mixed age or multi-age grouping refers to grouping children so that the age span of the class is greater than one year, as in the nongraded approach. Mixed-age and multi-age grouping emphasize the goal of teaching and curriculum practice use that makes maximum benefit of the cooperation and interaction of the children of various ages. In multi-age classes, teachers encourage the children with different ages of development and experience to help each other with all classroom activities including application and mastery of basic literacy and mathematical skills. But, teachers use small temporary subgroupings in mixed-age classes for children who require the same types of instruction that will help them get basic skills.

Implications of different age groupings

Grouping practices might seem to have slight distinctions but there are significant implications in practice. Ungraded or nongraded approaches indicate that age is not a good indicator of what children are ready to learn. It emphasizes regrouping children for class based on perceived readiness to acquire skills and knowledge instead of age. Its main goal is of homogenizing children for instruction for achievement rather than age even though this was not the original reasoning for the term. Groupings of combined grades and continuous progress practices do not intend to increase a sense of family within class or to encourage children to share knowledge and experience. But mixed-age grouping does take advantage of heterogeneity of experience and skills in a group of children.

Safe learning environment

One of the most effective points that can be made to help establish a safe learning environment for students is to help them learn that errors are friends rather than faults. Students often apologize for not knowing something. They can be reassured that no one knows everything and that everyone has something to learn. Teachers can teach them to value their correct answers rather than dwelling on the errors that they made. They have learned to count errors. They can be taught to count the number they got right, thus offering positive reinforcement. Even if a student gets one item correct and the remainder or incorrect, the student can be told that they have already learned something. Patterns of errors can be pointed out as well.

The numerous, well-publicized instances of violence in schools as well as society have prompted many schools to consider making violence prevention and conflict resolution as part of the curriculum. These programs rely on instruction that is ongoing and discussion that helps change the perceptions, skills and attitudes of children. A number of these curricula have been available since the 1980s. These include conflict resolution, violence prevention and curricula for solving social problems. These curricular approaches typically are integrated into a broader program that has other components such as peer mediation, cooperative learning, programs that address school wide behavior management as well as programs that are used to address anger management. Peer mediation uses a group of student mediators who are taught a negotiation procedure that is interest-based, along with problem-solving strategies and communication to help settle disagreements without confrontation or violent actions. Students come to mediation on a voluntary basis and are guided by the peer mediators to move from blaming each other to coming up with solutions that are acceptable to all parties. Peer mediation often is put in place as a part of a broader program for conflict resolution. Peer mediation can substantially change how students approach conflicts and settle them. Students who are involved in peer mediation often express a greater desire to help friends avoid fights and solve their problems.

Most incidents of school violence or serious disruption begin as less serious behavior that has escalated to the point of requiring attention. Many aggressive or disruptive behaviors that spiraled out of control could have been prevented by early and appropriate classroom responses. A well-documented knowledge base exists on how to prevent misbehavior escalation in the classrooms. A number of those programs have become available that integrate those findings into classroom management packages. Most rely on principles of effectively managing the classroom including:

- Multiple options that rely on various strategies and responses for maintaining an effective learning environment.
- Emphasizing the positive.
- Teaching responsibility.
- Decelerating emotional conflict.

- Consistency in behavior. What is appropriate behavior at school.
- Early responses that let the student know what the school and classroom rules are and that they will be enforced.

Many of those involved as perpetrators in the well-publicized school shootings in recent years had been picked on or persecuted by their peers. This highlights why addressing bullying in school is essential. Studies show that almost one-third of elementary students are bullied. About 10 percent of secondary school students have reported being bullied. But studies have also shown that school personnel persistently underestimate the extent of bullying that is in their school compared to the students. Students also worry no action will be taken. A whole-school approach may be needed to combat bullying rather than individual interventions. This could include awareness programs for teachers, parents and students. Also school and classroom policies are enforced helps send a clear message that there is no tolerance for bullying.

Little data exists showing that punitive zero tolerance policies have significantly improved school safety or student behavior. Researchers have begun to see what works and what does not in preventing school violence. The programs that seem to be most effective are proactive rather than reactive. These programs involve families, students, teachers and communities. They include a number of components that help address the complexity of school violence and disruption. There is far more data available supporting the effectiveness of bullying prevention programs, anger management or peer mediation programs than there is to support how well violence and disruption is stemmed by technological means such as surveillance cameras or metal detectors.

There are three assumptions underlying how schools can reduce the risk that minor incidents and disruptions will turn into life-threatening violence. These assumptions are:

- Violence is preventable. Serious violent incidents seem unpredictable. But prevention can make a difference. No guarantee exists that schools with comprehensive programs will be violence free. But schools that implement violence prevention components will see fewer incidents of disruption and can lower the chance of serious violence.
- There is no one quick fix. Many schools have begun the use of metal detectors in the wake of school shootings or have instituted no tolerance suspensions and expulsion. But no data exists to show the effectiveness of these measures.
- Prevention requires continuous planning and commitment. Effective school safety must have ongoing planning, commitment and partnerships between the school staff, parents and community.

Intrinsic and extrinsic motivation

Intrinsic motivation can be seen when people take part in an activity for its own sake, without some obvious external incentive present. An example is a hobby. Extrinsic motivation is the desire to perform a behavior that is based on the potential external rewards that the activity might bring. It was once thought that both intrinsic and extrinsic behavior were additive and could not be combined to form higher motivation levels. Some

scholars believe that students are more likely to experience intrinsic motivation if they:

- Attribute their educational results to internal factors they can control.
- Believe that they can be effective agents in reaching their goals.
- Are motivated by the deep mastery of a topic rather than rote learning just to get a grade.

Motivated readers

Motivated readers are those who generate their own literacy learning opportunities and while doing so they start to determine their own literacy learning destiny. This puts motivation as part of an engagement process. An engaged reader reads for different purposes, participates in social interactions that are meaningful around reading and scaffolds knowledge that helps construct new learning. Motivation can take place at any time with any young reader. Teachers can suggest to parents ways to motivate children to read at home even when the parent is busy and cannot drop what they are doing. One way to get the child another reading audience is to suggest that the child read to a few dolls or stuffed animals. This kind of activity can help both prereaders and beginning readers.

Enhancing comprehension

Reading comprehension

The process of learning to read is not a linear one. Students need not learn decoding before they learn to comprehend. Both skills should be taught at the same time beginning at the earliest stages of instruction for reading. Comprehension strategies can be taught using material that is read to children and the material that they read for themselves. Before reading, teachers can delineate the reason for the reading: vocabulary review, encouraging children to predict what stories are about or activating background knowledge. Teachers can direct children's attention to subtle or difficult portions of the text during reading, point out difficult words and ideas and ask children to find problems and solutions. After reading, children can be taught particular metacognitive strategies such as asking themselves regularly whether what is being read makes sense.

Oral communication

Guided oral reading
Guided oral reading is an instruction strategy that may help student improve various reading skills including fluency in reading. In general, a teacher, parent or peer will read a passage aloud and model fluent reading. Students then reread the text quietly, sometimes several times, on their own. The text should be at the student's level of independent reading. Students then read aloud and reread the same passage. Usually reading the text four times is plenty. More specific techniques include having an adult or peer reading with the student by modeling fluent reading and then asking the student if he or she will read the same passage aloud while being encouraged by the adult or peer.

Debate
Debate practices oral language skills and higher order thinking skills through an argument that is structured while discussing knowledge of content. The teacher must choose a topic which must be any question that can be answered with a yes or no. Or the topic may be stated as a resolution. The teacher may also choose one of several debate formats. They may be in the Webster-Hayne format in which students are divided into two teams of unlimited size with each side taking turns to speak. The Lincoln-Douglas, Kennedy-Nixon and academic debate are more formal, that allow two speakers each, a specific time period, a designated order and a time limit for speaking. Students are given a side to argue and they research material to support their side.

Written communication

Cooperative writing in second grade and beyond
Specific instruction in writing for different reasons and audiences as well as instruction in strategies to help clarify and enrich language expression is crucial. Language mechanical skills such as usage, capitalization and grammar can be taught and integrated into the students' own writing through the process of editing. Students might study, for instance, the use of adjectives and adverbs and then write descriptive compositions. Cooperative learning can be a very effective upper elementary reading and writing instruction if used properly. Students should generally work in groups of four to five members that stay together for six-to-eight weeks. The group might be presented a lesson on main idea and the students can work in groups to practice such a skill.

Writing prompts
Such a strategy could include a four-step process to help students in decision-making on their writing. It helps the students consider:
- The writer's role or voice.
- For whom the student is writing.
- The format used for writing the piece.
- The topic to be written about. The teacher can give examples for subjects such as social studies.

The students look over the four questions, consider the topic, then individually and in small groups, the use the process to plan their writing. Students can have various roles, formats and audiences. For a unit on World War II a role might be offered for an American, German or Japanese soldier, or a French resistance fighter. An audience might be self, community, government or home. Format could include letters, diary, speeches, or news articles or editorials.

Value boxes
Value boxes help students change from thinking to writing with graphic organizers preparing them to build written arguments. It categorizes and notes values that are associated with an idea in three areas: good, bad and interesting. Partners or small groups can meet to discuss ideas and add to lists which are then used to formulate writing. This strategy can be used to help answer higher level thinking questions that need reflection of historical decisions or the impacts of events in history. After writing positive, negative or interesting they would then write an expository essay with a thesis that evaluates the impact and argues points written in the value boxes.

Charts
A student can use charts to help develop a thesis when writing about history papers using charts that list the key events during a particular time period. The student would imagine how the story would seem in a movie and list scenes, locations that are crucial to the plot and then work with others to develop a list of key events in those locations and the moments and factors that contribute to how characters or situations evolve. This also may be displayed, compared and discussed as a continuing aid for understanding the story. The students will generate different hypotheses about the information found on the charts. All of the hypotheses are listed and students pick one or two that might help them in

writing. Students also share ideas in peer feedback groups.

Story organization
Writers look through drafts to find narrative elements that make their work even better. All the while they must consider the points they are trying to make. They ask what messages and themes exist. A rough draft can serve as an outline that lists statements central to a story. Sentences and paragraphs need to be carefully analyzed, no matter if you are writing fiction or nonfiction. Labeling paragraphs help to organize the story through the linkage of similar blocks of text. In news writing, reporters use the inverted pyramid model to organize a story from most important to least important information. This theoretically makes it easier in the editing process because editors know where to find the least important text. That is not always the case, however. Writers who are comparing or contrasting items may want a point-by-point or block-by-block approach to story organization.

Elementary school paper organization
Students writing their first papers must have organization schemes that will help them write with clarity and allow their teachers and peers to read with comprehension. Such a paper might begin with pre-writing, in which ideas are gathered, organized and brainstormed. A rough draft is then made. If the writing is done on a computer, making a copy and editing it might present the reader with a different perspective than that upon the screen. The paper then undergoes revision. The paper is read and reread in order to ensure that the paper makes sense. Details may be added that will make the paper more interesting. Text should be taken out that does not belong. Editing should be done in which checking occurs for capitalization, punctuation, spelling and other items such as subject-verb agreement. Changes may be

discussed with a peer or teacher. Finally, the paper is published.

Fifth grade news reporting literacy activity

Students are told to be reporters and report the news for their school. They are told they will need to report on local news, world news, national news, sports, entertainment and weather. The reporter should visit various news Web sites to gather information for the stories. The stories must be accurate, informative and interesting. The audience is the students' fifth grade class so it has to be in language they understand. The teacher functions as editor. The student learns the parts of the newspaper in this exercise: The headline, the lead, how to write a lead, quotes, body and ending. There should be pre-writing planning and collection of information. The student gets a "beat" and finds and writes the story.

Recursive strategies for composing texts

The framework for composing texts includes invention, drafting, revision and editing. Many recursive strategies lie inside these components. Invention refers to the ways a writer thinks about what he or she wants to do and how it might be done. It happens using outlines, seeking other opinions and perspectives and research. It is recursive in that writers invent throughout the act of writing, planning, revising and editing. Drafting refers to the different versions of a text before closure. Writers discover as a result of writing and draft then draft some more. Some view revision as writing, as a way to see the text from different perspectives. Revision also is rethinking ideas and how they may be conveyed. Editing refers to decisions that writers make to produce writing in which the words and punctuation are correct along with flowing sentence structure and diction.

Developmental process of writing

Writing is a process that is developmental. It requires teachers to give students more responsibility and to make decisions about topics, genre and collaboration whenever they are writing. Teachers who recognize writing as a process understand that:

- Writing is recursive. The writer moves within the components. Some writers might produce drafts during revision; others may naturally combine revision and editing.
- Both process and writing product should be evaluated and assessed to allow both student and teacher to focus on the learning taking place during writing rather from only the finished piece.
- The basic components of the writing are similar from person to person but each writer is unique and develops their own writing process.
- Writing abilities are mostly acquired by practice and frequent writing.
- Many writers attribute their skill to reading frequently.

Writing develops in stages from being dependent to becoming independent. The first stage is a novice who has little, if any, individual style. He or she is dependent on the teacher and seeks approval from the teacher. Stage 2 is a transitional writer. The writer needs support and coaching in order to develop. Learning is from modeled behaviors. Stage 3 is the willing writer who is able to collaborate with others and can learn from criticism. This writer enjoys practicing the craft and develops an appreciation for the audience. Stage 4 is the independent writer. This writer is autonomous, has developed a sophisticated personal style, has developed a writer's voice, is self-aware and is self-motivating.

Supporting and managing the writing process

Students who are at a middle level respond well to a classroom structure that is predictable while offering some choice and flexibility. It is important to develop an environment in which students can be encouraged to feel safe in taking risks in order to develop a sense of community of writers supporting and sharing with each other. The teacher is part of the community. The teachers should let students help to set rules and guidelines. Desks can be arranged in groups or tables can be used for several students. Resources can be provided on a specified shelf. These resources include dictionaries, language texts, literature for models and samples of writing by class members. Information on the writing process can be displayed on bulletin boards. The teacher can designate certain classroom areas for specific activities connected with writing.

Publishing student writing

Publishing a student's writing is a means of helping students look positively on literature. The student has his or her interest rewarded when published and it also boosts a child's confidence level. Publishing is a good way to help the student who is reluctant to write. This also helps children practice their writing and to develop their skills. Schools have traditionally had limited means of publishing student work, perhaps a student newspaper or an occasional literary journal. The feedback one gets writing in class may not bring the feelings that one would have seeing their work in print and read by others. But the Internet provides opportunities for publishing student work. There exist a number of sites on the Internet that specifically publish student work. Other ways to publish include the use of a class Web page or a weblog (blog).

Weblogs, usually called "blogs," are an easy way for students to have their work published. Students can have their own individual blogs or the class can have a blog that is contributed to by students. There are a number of considerations that should be thought about by the student before producing a blog since it is on the Internet. The students should consider what topics are appropriate to write about. Their teachers, parents and classmates can see their blogs as can total strangers. Students should think about topics with which they are comfortable. Students also should consider if the topics will be interesting. They need to think about who their audience will be: what details are needed and what type of background information is required for the audience.

There are several ways for creating publications for students within their classes including the use of the Internet along with developing hard-copy publications. This includes:

- Dividing classes into groups to produce a newsletter or some other publications. Newsletters are relatively simple to produce using the templates that come with many word processing programs.
- Assigning and electing an editorial board to be responsible for publishing.
- The teacher can be the editor who selects what will be published. Students submit their work to the teacher which he or she can organize to reflect goals of the class or topics that are covered. The copies of these publications can make the student proud.

Promoting vocabulary development

Technical vocabulary and language content strategy

A strategy for technical vocabulary and language development is a word category exercise requiring thinking on an interpretive level. A teacher will establish sets of four words in which three of the sets are related. Students circle the word that is not related. On a line at the top of the set they write a word or phrase that defines the relationship of the three words left. This is a way to comprehend historical terms in a manner other than through memorizing definitions and facts, and it forces the student to employ higher-level thinking. It can help to review and show a vocabulary understanding as well as information from a chapter or unit, or in marking periods using sets of historical people, places, ideas and events.

Teaching vocabulary

A vocabulary is a set of words that a person or other entity knows that are a part of language. A person's vocabulary is defined either as the set of all words that person understands or the set of all words the person is likely to use when constructing new sentences. How rich a person's vocabulary is most times is thought of as a reflection of intelligence or level of education. Increasing the size of one's vocabulary, or vocabulary building, is an important part of learning and improving one's skill in a language. Students in school are taught new words as part of a particular lesson. Many adults find vocabulary building enjoyable. Words help derive meaning from the text, which is the main goal in reading. Reading comprehension is needed for all subjects that a person learns. A deep vocabulary helps all readers better understand what is read.

Language expansion is the process of taking a verbalization used by a child and adding to it. Language modeling is the process of talking to children and narrating what occurs in their immediate environment. This involves the pairing of actions or objects with simple words in order to explain the purpose of those words. Language modeling and expansion give the child an opportunity to hear and learn language as well as allowing the child to hear the appropriate articulation and attempting to imitate sounds and combinations of sounds. Modeling and expansion is simple words or basic sentences that are easy to understand and have complex structures that are reduced. Most words are learned during everyday experiences with language. Interactions between children and adults are the best way for children to expand their vocabularies.

While much vocabulary is learned indirectly, some vocabulary needs to be directly taught. Direct instruction helps student learn words that are difficult such as those words representing concepts that are not part of the everyday experience of a student. The direct instruction of vocabulary in the case of a text leads to better comprehension. Direct instruction includes giving student word instruction that is specific and teaching students strategies for learning words. Specific word instruction can help expand a student's knowledge of word meanings. A deeper knowledge can help students understand what it is they are writing or speaking. Before reading texts, the teacher should teach them specific words that will appear in the text.

Extended instruction promotes active interaction with vocabulary which improves learning words. Children learn words best when instruction is provided over an extended time period and when the instruction has them working actively with the words. The more that the students use those new words, the more they will be used in different contexts which leads to them being more likely to learn the words. Repeated exposure to vocabulary in many contexts helps word learning. Students learn new words better when they see them often and in different contexts. The more that children hear, see and work with specific words, the better they can learn them. Students are given repeated exposure to new words when extended instruction is provided.

Here is an example of how to teach specific words in class. A teacher might have his class read a novel. The novel may have a concept that is important to the plot so the teacher might try several ways to ensure the students understand what that concept means. For instance, the teacher might get students to discuss the concept and read a sentence from the book that contains the concept, then ask students to use context and prior knowledge to try and determine what the concept means. The teacher might ask the students to use the concept word in their own sentences to help deepen the understanding of the word. Students need to develop word-learning strategies such as using dictionaries to help learn and understand word meanings or using information about word parts to figure out what a word in text means.

Extended and active instruction can be used to better learn words. A first-grade teacher wants their student to understand the concept of work. Over time, the teacher has the students do exercises in which they repeatedly use the meaning of the concept of work. The students have many opportunities to see and use the words in different contexts that will reinforce the meaning of the word. The teacher will ask them what they already know about work and have

them give example of the type of work their parents perform. The class could have a discussion about the work that is done at school. The teacher can find a simple book about work that introduces ideas about specific work that should be done. The teacher can ask students to make up sentences describing the work their parents do.

Repeated exposure to words can be taught in a manner such as this: A second-grade class is reading about George Washington. The story talks about his role as a farmer. The teacher wants to ensure the students understand the meaning of farm and farmer because both words are an important part of the book and because they are words students need to know in school and their everyday lives. The teacher calls the students' attention to the words farm and farmer when mentioned in textbooks and reading selections. The teacher has students use the word in their own writing. The teacher asks the students to find the words in print in newspapers. Upon reading the book, the teacher discusses George Washington's role as a farmer and how farms were different from today.

Knowing common prefixes and suffixes along with base and root words can help student learn the meanings of many words. Just learning the most common English prefixes (un-, re-, in-, dis-) gives students clues to more than half of all the English words with prefixes. Prefixes are relatively easy to learn because their meanings are clear. For instance, un- means not and re- means again. They usually are spelled similarly from word to word and they are always at the word's beginning. Suffixes can be more challenging to learn because their meanings are more abstract than prefixes. For instance, -ness means "the quality or state of" something. Other suffixes are easier to figure out such as -less which means without. Teachers should teach word roots as they occur in texts as well as teaching those root words that are most likely to be encountered.

Dictionaries and reference aids

Here is an example of how dictionaries and other reference material can be taught to learn vocabulary. A second-grade teacher finds that many of his students do not know the word "might" such as in the sentence: "The children moved the rock with all their might." The teacher shows them how to find the word "might" in the classroom dictionary and shows that there are five definitions for the word "might." The teacher reads each definition and discusses with the class whether each definition would fit in the sentence's context. The students eliminate the definitions of might that do not work in the sentence. The teacher then has students substitute the most likely definition for "might" in the original sentence to ensure it makes sense.

Dictionary game

A dictionary game is a team activity that can help students build their vocabularies and improve their dictionary skills. In the game, the student teams first compete against each other to find word definitions in the dictionary. The team that is the fastest reads the word definition, tells what part of speech the word is and correctly uses the word in a sentence. Other teams can challenge the team's response. Points are given for correct answers or challenges. The value of this game is in it demonstrating the difference between the primary definition of a word and its specific use in context of a particular content area or in reading. Students may quickly learn that the primary definition of a word is not necessarily going to be its meaning in specific contexts.

Context clues

Here is an example of how to use context clues to determine the meaning of a vocabulary word. A student reads a sentence: "The birds were chirping loudly and the cat was quickly tiring of the racket. The cat quickly became unhappy with the birds. The cat finally solved the problem when it accidentally stuck its head into a bowl and was not able to hear a thing." The teacher tells the students that the context of the paragraph helps to determine what racket means. There is chirping and it is loud. The cat was unhappy. When the cat got its head stuck in a bowl it could no longer hear the chirping. These are all clues that the birds are being noisy and that racket means loud noise.

Indirect instruction

Indirect instruction of vocabulary can be encouraged in two major ways. First, students should be read to no matter what grade level. Students of all ages can learn words from hearing texts being read to them. Reading aloud is most efficient as a means of indirect teaching when the teacher discusses the selection with the class before, during and after the selection is read. The teacher should talk with students about the new vocabulary words and concepts, and help them relate the words to their prior experiences and knowledge. Another way to indirectly teach vocabulary words is to encourage students to read expansively on their own. The students should be encouraged to read on their own during independent work sessions.

Choosing words to teach

A teacher will most likely have the ability to teach maybe eight to ten new words per week so the words that are to be taught most be chosen carefully. The focus should be on teaching:

- Important words. When words are taught to before students read a text, the words that are important to understanding concepts in the text should be taught directly. The students may not know several other words in the selection but there will not be time to teach them all.
- Useful words. Words should be taught that the student will likely see and use many times.
- Difficult words. Some instruction should be given on words that are difficult for the students. Particular challenges include words with multiple meanings depending on in what context they are used.
- Plan and implement instruction addressing strengths and needs.

Word knowledge

Knowledge of words by a student is not a matter of them knowing or not knowing those words. Instead, the words are known to certain degrees. They may not have seen or heard a word before. They may have heard it or seen it but only vaguely knows what that word might mean. Or they may be very familiar with a word meaning and be able to accurately use it in speech and writing. The three levels of word knowledge are known as unknown, acquainted and established. At the unknown level, the word is completely unfamiliar and meaning is not known. At acquainted, the word is somewhat familiar and there is some idea of meaning. At the established level, the word is very familiar, can be easily recognized and can be used correctly.

Types of word learning

There are four different types of word learning that have been identified: learning a new meaning for a known word; learning the meaning for a new word that represents a known concept; learning the meaning of a new word representing an unknown concept; and clarifying and enriching the meaning of a known word. These different kinds of word learning have various levels of difficulty. Perhaps one of the most common and most challenging is learning the meaning of a new word that represents an unknown concept. This type of word learning is needed for learning in content areas. Learning words and concepts in mathematics, social studies and science particularly can be challenging because each concept often is associated with other concepts.

Word consciousness

Students can be helped to better develop their vocabularies when teachers foster word consciousness. Word consciousness is an awareness and an interest in words, the meanings of those words and the power of the word. Word-conscious students know many words and are able to use them correctly. Students can enjoy words and can be eager to learn new words. They also know how to learn them. Teachers can help students develop word consciousness in several ways. A teacher can call their attention to the ways authors choose words to express meanings. Students can be encouraged to engage in word play, such as puns. Teachers can help them research the origin or history of a word. Teachers can also encourage the students to look for examples of a word's usage in their daily lives.

Word analogies

Word analogies can be used to let students connect familiar words and concepts with new ideas and prior experiences with new information. In such a strategy, the student can confront two words which are related and then is challenged to explain the nature of their relationship. Next, the students apply the same relationship to other pairs of words. The form for a word analogy exercise is typically: "Term A is to Term B as Term C is to what word?" Students display critical thinking on two levels using this exercise. First, they describe the relationships between the firs pair of words and then suggest new word pairs with similar relationships.

Learning environment

Culturally responsive teaching

One goal of effective teaching is making learning a meaningful endeavor for children. Children must see connections between what they know and what they experience in schools and other settings in order to comprehend their experience. Increasing the congruence and continuity between children's home and school environments is a crucial aspect in achievement for children who come from diverse cultures and varied social classes. Recognizing and fostering the cultural knowledge of children from culturally and linguistically diverse backgrounds can help bridge the gap between home and school. Creating a culturally responsive learning situation takes a lot of work. This includes effective partnerships between schools and families where each a treated as a full partner in attaining a successful outcome.

Needs and practices across content areas

Studies have shown that it is impossible to separate practices in the classroom such as strategies for activating prior knowledge from the larger cultural and social contexts in which the practices exist. Researchers say a need exists for adolescent literacy that includes adolescent's literacy practices beyond the confines of the classroom setting, their expanded conceptions of text such as the Internet and the relationship that exists between the development of identity and literacy. However, the need for additional research in teaching and learning of context in secondary schools still exists. For instance, more study is needed on the interactions of the student and teacher, of student and student, how students perceive themselves as readers, what their interests are at a particular time and how institutional configurations affect the daily events occurring both in and out of school.

Emphasis on content areas

Attention should be paid to literacy in content areas for several reasons. The 2003 National Assessment of Educational Progress Reading Report shows that general test scores have improved over recent years but very few youngsters in the United States can read at proficient or advanced levels. Most can decode and answer simple comprehension questions but few can synthesize ideas, interpret the information they receive or critique the ideas they read about, especially when they work with expository texts. Also, literacy in content areas has consequences that go beyond the ability to understand a subject-matter text. Advanced or specialized literacy forms are tools that signify success in both school and socially and can be important for economic, social and political success beyond school.

Metadiscursive

Research shows that teaching in content areas should include teaching students to be metadiscursive, which means they should not only be able to be part of many different discourse communities but should also know why and how it is that they are taking part as well as what those engagements mean for them and others in the realm of larger power relationships and social position. That does not mean that the historical limitations in integrating content literacy should be ignored. Teaching content literacy still should focus on the knowledge and beliefs of students and teachers. This requires looking at questions such as: How do teachers work with a notion of subject-matter literacy as a metadiscursive practice while encountering probable resistance from students who have become comfortable with the notion that content area learning is a matter of rote memory and information reproduction?

Approaches to technological content

In order for students to ask the right questions about a subject they need background knowledge. Activating prior knowledge and then building upon that knowledge is a big concern for teachers. Teachers can use language arts strategies to helps students with ways to know what they know, what they should know and how to visualize content. With such a perspective, teachers can connect the focus on content in the curriculum in order to gain more general literacy strategies that students experience elsewhere. Teachers also are concerned with a lack of comprehension. Students often show a lack of deep conceptual understanding. One challenge is to design ways to help students become more skillful in what they do not know so that understanding can be used in supporting learning.

A curriculum that is project-based starts with explicit questions meant to stimulate the curiosity of students and serve as a basis for launching ideas for various research directions. Teachers can see that curricular units have a real advantage in motivating students insofar as developing hypotheses, finding research information in many sources of data to confirm or argue the hypotheses, and in developing arguments that are based in understanding concepts. The Internet can provide a wealth of information but provides challenges as well for teaching. Students with literacy challenges have difficulties finding information, identifying relevant information and then reading what they find. These challenges may sometime be linked to the inability of a student to draw conceptual parallels in content and then translating them into an Internet search.

Scaffolding

As proposed by Lev Vygotsky as part of his Social Cultural learning model, scaffolding is the process in which an adult/teacher provides help to a child then decreases the level of assistance as the child masters the skill or topic. Scaffolding ties in with what Vygotsky termed the Zone of Proximal Development (ZPD), which is the gap between what an individual knows about a topic and what he does not. In children, ZPD refers to the range of tasks a child can do with help from a parent or teacher but which he cannot accomplish on his own. A teacher can use scaffolding and awareness of ZPD in planning lessons involving reading, writing, speaking, and listening. Specifically, a teacher reading out loud provides students with an opportunity to model that behavior, and then to write and read further about the topic, perhaps through the utilization of a KWL chart.

Dramatic activities as scaffolding
Elementary and English as a Second Language classes can use dramatic activities as scaffolding for effective literacy teaching. Researchers have found that scaffolded play with students of elementary age allow them to participate in language learning in an active way. Students may also be more motivated to

discuss, organize, rewrite and perform in the dramatic presentation. Students have also become more engaged in which there were interwoven activities involving literature, drama, music and movement, even for at-risk students in grades K-3. Activities involving bilingual children in which their own cultural experiences are called upon and valued. This also helps motivate and support literacy and meaningful learning environments.

Reciprocal teaching

Reciprocal teaching is in many ways the aggregation of four separate comprehension strategies, which are summarizing, questioning, clarifying and predicting. Summarizing presents the ability to identify and integrate the information that is most important in a text. Text can be summarized across sentences and paragraphs and across passages. When students start the reciprocal teaching procedures they are usually focused at sentence and paragraphs. Questioning reinforces the strategy of summarizing. When students identify questions they identify a kind of information that is important enough to provides substance for a question then post the information in question form. Clarifying is important for students with comprehension difficulty. They are taught to be alert to the effects of comprehension impediments and take the measures to restore meaning. Predicting is when student predict what the author will discuss next in the text.

Most important in reading education is turning out readers who can understand the meaning in texts. Reciprocal teaching is a scaffolded discussion technique built upon for ways that good readers can comprehend text through questioning, clarifying, summarizing and predicting. Teaching the students the four strategies helps give the student tools that great readers use in meeting their text-reading goals. Thus, the four strategies are what are taught rather than reading skills. These multiple strategies help students to read by giving them a choice of strategies that they can use in reading. The scaffolding gives support to help the students connect what they know and can do with what they need to do in order to be successful at learning a particular lesson. This also helps give the students a chance to support each other and foster a sense of community among classmates.

The word "reciprocal" in reciprocal teaching is somewhat misleading in that it does not entail students doing the teaching. But the students do get to use a set of four strategies -- summarizing, clarifying, predict and questioning -- to better improve reading comprehension. That improvement is the ultimate goal. The other goals include:

- The teacher scaffolds instruction of the strategy by guiding, modeling and applying the strategies.
- It guides students to become metacognitive and reflective in the use of strategies.
- It helps students monitor their comprehension of reading.
- It uses the social nature of learning in order to improve and scaffold the comprehension of reading.
- The instruction is presented through different classroom settings including whole group, guided reading groups and literature circles.

The order of the four stages of reciprocal teaching is not of great importance. A teacher will want to try out various ways to employ the strategy in order to see if a particular sequence fits a teaching style and the students' learning style. One also wants to carefully choose text selections so that they all fit in with the four stages of reciprocal teaching. Before successfully implementing reciprocal teaching, the students need to have been taught the four strategies as well as had ample opportunities to use them. One approach could be having students work from a chart with four columns. Each column will be headed by the different comprehension activity that is involved. Then put students in groups of four. Distribute one note card to each group member that tells the member's unique role of: summarizer, questioner, clarifier, predictor.

A reciprocal teaching exercise could operate using four-column charts, groups of four students with each playing a specific part of summarizer, questioner, clarifier and predictor. The students would have their defined role on a note card. The students then could read several paragraphs of the assigned text passage. They should be encouraged to use note-taking strategies such as selective underlining or sticky notes in helping for their role in the discourse. At a given stopping point, the summarizer will give the key ideas up to this particular point in the text. The questioner will then ask questions about the text such as unclear parts, puzzling information, connections to concepts that have already been learned or motivations of the characters or actors. The clarifier will try to clear up the confusing parts and answer questions that were asked. The predictor may make guesses about what the author might tell next. The roles then switch one person to the right and another selection is read.

Application of Theoretical & Knowledge Bases of Reading in Diagnosis & Assessment

Principles of reading assessment

Assessment systems

Assessment systems may include those that are norm-referenced, criterion-referenced, alternative assessments or classroom assessments. Criterion-referenced systems are those where an individual's performance is compared to a certain learning objective of performance standard and not based on the performance of other students. Norm-referenced systems are those where student performance is compared to a larger, "norm group," which may be a national sample that represents a diverse cross-section of students. These tests usually sort student and measure achievement towards some performance criterion. An individual assessment is one focusing on the individual student such as a portfolio assessment. This is a portfolio of the students' classroom work. Alternative assessments are those requiring students to respond to a question rather than a set of responses.

Wide-Range Achievement Test

The Wide-Range Achievement Test is one of a number of standardized achievement assessments to determine a child's cognitive ability. It is for individuals ages 5-75. It contains scoring for reading, spelling and math. It provides up to 30 minutes for each of the three forms. The test uses a single-level format as well as alternative forms. These alternative forms may be used with one another in order to provide a more qualitative assessment of academic skills, or leaving the other form for testing at a later time. The reading subtest includes letter naming and word pronunciation out of context. The spelling subtest asks the student to write his or her own name and then write words as they are directed. The mathematical portion includes counting, reading problems, number symbols and written computation.

Formative assessment

A formative assessment is a diagnostic use of assessment to provide feedback to teachers and students over the course of instruction. That is in contrast to a summative assessment, which usually happens after a period of instruction and requires making judgments about the learning that has occurred such as with a test score or paper. Assessments in general include teacher observation, classroom instruction, or an analysis of student work including homework and tests. Assessments are formative when the information is used to adapt teaching and learning to meet the needs of the student. When teachers know how students are progressing and where they are having difficulties, they can use this information to make needed instructional adjustments such as reteaching, alternative instruction approaches or offering more practice opportunities.

The goal of formative assessment is to gain an understanding of what students know or don't know in order to make responsive changes in teaching and learning. So techniques such as teacher observation and classroom discuss have an important place along analyzing tests and homework. Questioning and classroom discussion is a good way to increase the students' knowledge and improve understanding. The teacher does need to make sure to ask thoughtful, reflective questions instead of those that are simple, factual ones and give students sufficient time to respond. Students might be invited to discuss their thinking about a question in small groups. Several possible answers could be provided and let students vote on them. Or students could be asked to write down an answer then read a selected few out loud.

Informal assessment

Although there is no uniformly accepted definitions for formal and informal assessments, informal can mean techniques that are easily put into classroom routines and learning activities to measure a student's learning outcome. Informal assessment can be used without interfering with instructional time. The results can be an indicator of the skills or subjects that interest a student. They do not provide comparison to a broader group like standardized tests. Informal tests require clear understanding of the levels of a student's abilities. Informal assessments seek identification of a student's strength and weaknesses without a regard to norms or grades. Such assessments may be done in structured and unstructured manners. Structured ones include checklists or observations. Unstructured assessments are those such as student work samples or journals.

Performance assessments

Performance assessments can be used to document and evaluate the work done by students during a fixed time period. These assessments tend to take the form of lengthy, multidisciplinary problem-solving activities. Teaching and learning with performance assessments should be documented and assessed with tools based on performance of real tasks. Students should have the opportunities to exhibit their expertise before family and community. Performance assessments may be short-answer or extended responses. They include oral questions, traditional quizzes, open-ended prompts and tests.

Implementing literacy assessment

Informal reading inventory

The informal reading inventory is an individually administered survey that is designed to help determine a student's needs in reading. The student's performance on the informal reading inventory will help to determine the instructional level and the amount and kind of support the student is likely to need. Specifically, using the informal reading inventory will help you assess a student's strengths and needs in the areas of word recognition, word meaning, reading strategies and comprehension. An informal reading inventory is a suitable tool for determining a student's ability to read and his or her needs, it is not infallible. An educator should use information from the inventory along with other tests and information to make decisions about instructional plans.

Once written comprehension questions are chosen, a teacher will want to determine the number of errors that are permissible for the students. Students are often scored in three ways: independent (can read on their own), instructional (could read if classroom help is available) and frustration (the student will most likely find this piece too difficult even in a classroom setting). Where the child falls on that scale depends upon the amount of errors per 100 words that the student commits. For example, some approximate score able errors allowed on a particular piece might be one or two errors per 100 words for an independent reader and scores 90 percent or higher on comprehension questions.

To administer a student reading inventory certain materials would be needed such as a stop watch to time the student, a copy of all readings for the student, a copy of all readings and comprehension questions for scoring purposes. Step one would be to explain to students that this is not a test. Tell them that this inventory is really to tell how the teacher can teach them better. Next, set the timer. Step 3, Begin the timer as the student reads the first excerpt aloud. Next, score errors on the teacher's copy. Step 5, Stop the timer when the student stops. Record the total time. Give the comprehension questions and record the answers.

On-demand writing assessment

An on-demand writing assessment for a ninth-grader might embed stages of the writing process into defined time periods. Students write about events from their past. The prompt focuses on some aspect of the social or intellectual development of the students. The topic is to encourage ninth grade students to be reflective. An example topic might be when the student got into a new interest, or to describe a book or TV show that had a particularly strong effect on what they did or thought. The assessment includes the task introduction, a short reading selection that serves as a model, some discussion questions, one or more planning suggestion, a prompt and a checklist of revision and editing questions.

Group reporting

Group reporting is a fun way for students to show the teacher and their peers what they have learned. Small groups are used with students interacting with each other. The students also learn from each other and use social skills. Groups that work

together consistently may create a portfolio of the group work. This could include self-assessments where the students can comment on what they have learned creating the portfolio. A group skit is a creative way to demonstrate almost anything the students have learned. A mini-fair is another activity where, after a small group project, the students can share it with booths in a location where other class members can see it.

Rubrics

Rubrics are a set of assessment criteria that specifies the characteristics, knowledge and competencies indicating a student's level of achievement. It is basically a list of characteristics that are used to assess a learning product's quality. Rubrics identify traits and components that indicate to what extent a learning outcome has been achieved. Rubrics are often used to attach authentic meaning to both letter and number grades. Rubrics also offer advantages such as:

- Rubrics allow students to document the grade they earned rather than the grade given or assigned.
- Tests and research papers may not offer a valid reflection of learning outcomes while rubrics are tied to learning outcomes.
- Grades alone offer limited reflections of a student's learning.

Questioning techniques

Key questions should be planned to give direction and structure to the lesson. Spontaneous questions that come up are fine but the overall direction of the discussion has been mostly planned. Here are some simple guidelines to asking questions that will help teacher's questioning skills:

- Be sure the question is clear. Think about what it is required from the student before asking the question.
- Frame the question without calling on a particular student. Students are free to ignore the question when a student is called upon before the question is asked.
- After framing the question, pause while the students have a chance to think of an answer and then call on a student to respond. This pause, called wait time, is an important questioning skill. A wait time between a question and asking for response should be between 2-4 seconds.

Surveys

Surveys help gather information of any type whether specific names need to be attached are do not need to be detached. Surveys are good in determining what a student feels about the instruction. They may be used in order to determine the level of knowledge on various issues related to the content that is being studied. This could help provide a baseline of where the students are. Surveys that are similar can then be given at later periods of time to determine what they have learned. Surveys are good in determining how the student feels about what he or she has learned in the class from their point of view. Rather than from a standardized test score that shows academic outcomes, surveys can provide a more personal level of knowledge that the student may have gained from the class.

Constructed-response tests

Constructed-response tests are a non-multiple choice type of exam that requires some type of written or oral response. Selected-response tests are questions from predetermined list of answers that include multiple choice, true/false, matching or fill in the blanks questions. Each type of test has its benefits. Selected-response formats allow more questions to be asked in shorter time periods. Scoring is faster and it is easy to create comparable test forms. Since selected-response tests can normally be answered quickly, more items that covers several content areas can be administered in a short period of time. They also can be machine-scoreable tests that allow quicker and more objective scoring. Constructed-response tests have the potential for gathering deeper information about a student's knowledge and understanding of a content area. Constructed-response items are more time consuming and allow fewer items to be covered.

Miscue analysis

A miscue analysis is an assessment in which a child reads a story aloud and the teacher checks for errors in the recognition and comprehension of words. Such an analysis might be performed in the following manner:

- The teacher instructs the student they will read a passage aloud without the teacher's help.
- A videotape or audiotape should be made for analysis after the session.
- After reading the teacher marks all miscues, including insertions, mispronunciations, omissions and corrections by the student.
- The teacher records the miscues by writing what the text said in one column and what the reader said in another.
- The miscues are analyzed using criteria including whether the miscue went with the preceding context or was the miscue corrected.

- Percentages are calculated based on the total number of miscues.

Student work samples

Teachers can construct an assessment rubric by collecting a range of student work samples that all respond to the same skill and performance assessment. The teacher begins constructing the rubric by collecting a small range of work samples that do not necessarily respond to the same performance and skill assessment. The teacher then decides the assessment criteria for the rubric. The teacher then groups together related words or phrases to define each stack of work samples. The teacher clearly defines the terms and goals of the assessment in the rubric. The students are actively involved in developing the assessment measurements for the rubric with the teacher. The teacher makes known the expectations for the rubric. The teacher considers the forms of assessment used to evaluate student work.

Observation

Observation is one of the most powerful techniques that a teacher has. The purpose is to build a picture of a student's personal, social and cognitive development and how they are making progress in their learning. Only when a number of cameos, vignettes, snapshots, notes or indicators exist can teachers start looking for patterns in student behavior and make judgments about their performance. Dating such records will help record the contexts along with observed achievement characteristics in order to build a historical profile that is useful. In order to supporting and acknowledging students working at different levels, the teacher must exhibit flexibility and tailoring to the individual student. The formats should suit the particular activities, reflect the activities'

goals and support the recording of students working at different levels and rates.

Anecdotal records

Anecdotal records are written records kept in a positive tone of a child's progress that is based on milestones particular to the child's emotional, physical, aesthetic and cognitive development. They include specific dates, times and events of incidents throughout the school day. Some teachers use notebooks for such tasks while others use sticky pads. Sometimes the notes will become part of the child's file at the end of the year; they stay with the teacher's records or go in the trash. Anecdotal records are useful in parent conferences when a teacher explains how a child is doing. They also help keep track of a student's behavior. Keeping such records is useful in supporting why and how a teacher makes decisions.

Appropriate uses of assessment

Bias in selecting tests

When selecting tests, care should be taken to ensure the test is not biased or offensive with regard to race, sex, native language, geographic region or ethnic origin as well as other factors. Those who develop tests are expected to show sensitivity to the test-takers' demographic. Steps can be taken during test development and documentation to minimize the influence of cultural factors on the test scores. These may include evaluating the items for offensiveness, cultural dependency and using statistics to identify differential item difficulty. Questions to ask include: Were the tests analyzed statistically for bias? What method was used? How were the items selected for the final version? Should the test be used with non-native English speakers?

Authentic assessment

Authentic assessment asks students to apply their skills and knowledge the same way that they would be used in real-world situations. It is a performance-based assessment that requires each student to exhibit his or her in-depth knowledge and understanding through a mastery demonstration. It is an assessment of authentic learning which is the type of learning in which activities and materials are framed in real-life contexts. The underlying assumption of such an approach is that the material is meaningful to students and thus more motivating and processed deeply. Some of the terms or concepts that are related to authentic learning include contextual learning and theme-based curriculum.

Multiple assessments

Multiple assessment methods give a comprehensive view of whether students are achieving the learning outcome that a program identifies. A quantitative assessment lets educators provide numerical evidence of student learning while qualitative measures show a descriptive evidence of what the student has learned. Selecting the appropriate assessment method is dependent upon outcomes of student learning. For instance, if students complete a program and should have knowledge of the discipline, the knowledge would be best measured by a carefully constructed quantitative assessment. But if students are expected to use multiple perspectives when solving a problem the evidence might be better provided in some written form and examined in a qualitative manner by using scoring rubrics.

Portfolio assessments

Portfolios can be thought of as a scrapbook or photo album that records the progress and activities of the program and those who participate in it. It showcases them to interested parties both inside and outside of the program. Portfolios can be used to examine and measure progress by documenting the learning as it takes place. They extend beyond test scores to include a substantive picture of what a student is doing and experiencing. Portfolios are useful in documenting progress in higher-order goals such as applying skills and synthesizing experience beyond what standardized or norm-based tests do. The portfolio contents are sometimes known as "evidence" or "artifacts." They can include drawings, writing, photos, video, audio tapes computer discs and copies of program-specific or standardized tests.

Portfolio assessment is best used for the following:

- Evaluating programs with flexible or individualized outcomes or goals.
- Allowing individuals and programs in the community to be involved in their own change and decisions to change.
- Giving information that provides a meaningful insight into behavioral change
- Providing tools to ensure communications and accountability to a wide range of audiences. These participants such as families or community members may not be sophisticated in interpreting statistical data and can better appreciate more visual or experiential evidence of success being achieved.
- They allow for the possibility of assessing some of the more

important and complex aspects of many constructs.

Portfolio assessments are not as useful for the following:

- Evaluating programs that have very concrete, uniform purposes or goals. For instance, it would not be necessary to compile a portfolio for programs such as immunizing children by the age of five because the immunizations are the same and the evidence is usually straightforward and clear.
- Allowing a teacher to rank participants or a program in a quantitative or standardized way, even though evaluators or staff members of the program might be able to make subjective judgments or merit that is relative.
- Comparing participants or programs to standardized norms. Portfolios can and often do include some kinds of standardized test scores along with other types of evidence. However, this is not the main purpose in using portfolio assessments.

The advantages of using portfolio assessments include:

- Allowing evaluators to see the student or group as individual with unique characteristics, needs and strengths.
- Provides for future analysis and planning by showing a total pattern of an individual's strength, weaknesses or barriers to success.
- Serves as a concrete communication vehicle and provides ongoing communication or information exchange for those involved.
- Promotes ownership. Participants and groups can take an active role

in where it is they have been and where they would like to go.
- Offers the possibility of addressing the limitations of traditional assessments. It offers a possibility of assessing more complex and important facets of a topic or area.
- Covers a broad scope of information and knowledge, from different people who know the program or person in a different context.

Portfolio assessment has these disadvantages:

- It can be very time-intensive for teachers to evaluate, especially if the portfolios must be done in addition to traditional grading and tests.
- Having to develop individualized criteria may be unfamiliar or difficult at first.
- The portfolio could just be a collection of miscellaneous artifacts that does not show growth or progress if the goals and criteria for the programmatic are unclear.
- As is the case with other forms of qualitative data, the data that is used from portfolio assessments can be difficult to analyze or to aggregate in order to see progress or change in the individual student.

The main factors that guide the design and development of a portfolio are:

- Purpose. The primary concern is understanding the purpose that is to be served with the portfolio. This will define guidelines for collecting materials. For instance, is the goal to report progress? To identify special needs? For program accountability? For all such reason?

- Assessment criteria. The next decision to make is about the criteria standards or what will be considered a success, and what strategies are needed to meet the goals. Items are then selected to provide evidence of meeting the criteria or making progress with goals.
- Evidence. A number of considerations in collecting data are needed. What are the sources of evidence? How often should evidence be collected? How can sense be made of the evidence?

Many portfolio assessments exist but most fall into two types: process and product portfolios. Process portfolios document growth over time toward a goal. This documentation includes statements of end goals, criteria and future plans. Included should be baseline information or items used to describe a participant's performance or mastery of at the beginning of the program. Other items may be selected at different interim pints to demonstrate the steps toward mastery. Produce portfolios include examples of the best efforts of a group or participant. These include final evidence, or items which demonstrate that end goals are achieved. They can encourage reflection about learning or change. It can help to show a sense of strength and ownership and to showcase or communicate a person's accomplishments.

Portfolios used for assessment have certain essential characteristics including:
- Having multiple data sources including both people and artifacts. People can be teachers, participants or community members. Artifacts can be test scores, drawings, writings, videotapes and audiotapes.
- Having authentic evidence that is related to program activities.
- Being dynamic and capturing change and growth. Portfolios should include different stages of mastery which will allow a much deeper understanding of the change process.
- Being explicit in that participants should know what is expected of them.
- Being integrated, meaning having the evidence to establish a connection between program activities and life experiences.
- Being based on ownership, or the participant helping to determine evidence to include the goals that are to be met.
- Being multipurposed, or allowing for assessment of effectiveness of the program while assessing the performance of the participant.

Running records

Running records give teachers an important tool for making decisions on appropriate grouping, materials and support records when taken over time in early literacy training. They are based on structured observations of children's reading and writing behaviors and exemplify authentic assessment which is critical with emergent readers as they come across new reading material. The student reads from a text and the teacher watches closely, coding behaviors on a sheet of paper. Words that are accurately read are given a check. Errors receive a line with reader behaviors recorded above the line and teacher actions recorded below. A goal of the running records for this level would be to help students develop a "self-extending" system, which indicates that children learn to apply strategies of self-monitoring and self-correction on more difficult texts for extended amounts of text.

Certain points should be remembered when taking and scoring running records. These include:

- Running records must be analyzed to offer data for instructional uses in addition to being scored.
- Consider what text the student read, up to and including the error when analyzing a substitution.
- Do not make professional judgments based on the results of one running record. Reviewing the analysis and accuracy of scores of a number of running records is the only way to understand a student's reading process.
- Individual errors are studied for gaining insight into the reader's process.
- When analyzing a record, circle the cues that the reader used and not the ones that were neglected.

Validity and reliability

A test is valid when it measures what it is supposed to measure. How valid a test is depends on for what purpose it is used. For instance, a thermometer might measure temperature but it cannot measure barometric pressure. A test is reliable when it yields results that are consistent. A test may be reliable and valid, valid or not reliable, reliable and not valid or neither valid nor reliable. A test must be reliable for it to measure validity. The validity of a test is constrained by its reliability. If a test does not consistently measure a construct or domain then it may not be expected to have a high degree of validity.

Types of test validity include:

- Face validity. It begs the question: Does the test measure what should be measured?
- Content validity. This asks: Is the full content of a concept being defined being included in the measure? It includes a broad sample of what is tested, emphasizes material that is important and requires skills that are appropriate.
- Criterion validity. This asks: "Is the measure consistent with what is already known and expected?" There are two subcategories which are predictive and concurrent.
- Predictive validity predicts a known association between the construct being measured and something else.
- Concurrent validity is associated with indicators that pre-exist or something that already measures the same concept.
- Construct validity. This shows the measure that relates to a number of other measures that are specified.
- Discriminant validity. This type does not associate with unrelated constructs.

Some conventional views on test validity in recent years include:

- Face validity. This means a test is valid at face value. Psychometricians traditionally, as a check on face validity, sent test items to teachers for modification. This was abandoned for a long time because of its vagueness and subjectivity. But face validity returned in the 1990s in another form, with a definition that means validity as making common sense, being persuasive and appearing right to the reader.

- Content validity. This draws inferences from test scores to a large domain of items that are similar to those on a test. The concern with content validity is a sample-population representation, in that the knowledge and skills covered by the test should be representative of the larger knowledge and skill domain.

Factors affecting how valid a test is by itself include:
- History. Outside events that happen during the course of what is being studied may influence the results. It does not make the test less accurate.
- Maturation. Change due to aging or development between or within groups may affect validity.
- Instrumentation. The reliability is questioned because of a calibration change in a measuring device or changes in human ability to measure difference such as fatigue or experience.
- Testing. Test-taking experience affects results. This refers to either physical or mental changes, the attitude of a participant, or a physiological response by a participant may change after measures that are repeated.
- Statistical regression. This is the tendency to regress towards mean which makes scores higher or lower. If a measure is not reliable, some variation will occur between measures that are repeated.
- Selection. Participants in a group may be alike in certain ways so they will respond in different ways to the independent variable.
- Mortality. Participants drop out of a test, which makes the group

unequal. Who drops out and why also can be a factor.
- Interaction. Two or more threats can interact such as selection-maturation when there is a difference between age groups causing groups to change at different ages.
- Contamination. This is when a comparison group is in some way affected by or impacts another group which causes an increase of efforts. This is also called "compensatory rivalry."

Two particular threats to causing test invalidity are known as "construct under representation" and "construct-irrelevant variance." The first term indicates that the task being measured in the assessment fails to include discussions or facets of the construct which are important. So, the test results will like show a student's true abilities within the construct which was indicated as having been measured by the test. The second term means that a test measures too many variables. Many of these variables are irrelevant to the interpreted construct. This can take two forms "Construct irrelevant easiness" happens when outside clues in formats permit some individuals to respond correctly or appropriately in irrelevant ways to the assessed construct. "Construct-irrelevant difficulty" is when outside aspects make it difficult for individuals to respond correctly that make the task irrelevantly difficult for an individual or groups.

Regression analysis can be used to establish validity of the criteria of a test. An independent variable may be used as a predictor variable and a dependent variable which is the criterion variable. The correlation coefficient between them is known as the validity coefficients. For instance, test scores of a test is the criterion variable. It is hypothesized that if the student passes the test, he or she would meet the criteria of knowing the specific subject matter. Criterion validity values prediction over explanation. Predication is concerned with mathematical or non-casual dependence where as explanation pertains to casual or logical dependence. For instance, one can predict the weather based on the mercury height in a thermometer. The mercury could satisfy the criterion validity as a predictor. Yet one cannot say why the weather changes because the mercury's height.

Tests are reliable if they yield results that are consistent. They types of reliability include:

- Inter-observer. These yield consistent results among testers who are rating the same information.
- Test-retest. This is a measure of two different times with no treatment in between yielding results that are the same.
- Parallel-forms. These are two tests with different forms supposedly testing the same material and yielding the same results.
- Split-half reliability. This is when items are divided in half such as odd versus even questions and the two halves provide the same results. For all forms of reliability, a measurement of reliability that is quantitative can be used.

Views in recent decades on test reliability include:

- Temporal stability. This refers to the same form of testing on two or more separate occasions to the same group of students. This is not practical as repeated measurements are likely to result in higher scores on later tests after adopting the format.

- Form equivalence. This is relative to two different test forms based on the same content that is administered once to the same students.
- Internal consistency. This relates to the coefficient of test scores obtained from a single test. When no pattern is found in the student responses, the test is probably too difficult and students just randomly guess at the answers.
- Reliability is a needed but not sufficient condition for a test to be valid. The test might reflect consistent measurement but it is might not be especially valid.

Some scholars and testing experts say that performance, portfolio and responsive evaluations -- where tasks vary greatly from student to student and where multiple tasks may be simultaneously evaluate -- are not reliable. A difficulty cited is that there are many sources of errors in measuring performance assessment. For instance, a writing skill test score might have its reliability affected by raters or other factors. There may also be confusion about diversity of reliability indices. Nonetheless, different reliability measures share common thread. A replication is constituted in measurement procedures in situations such as internal consistency. The measure is used for convenience in computing the reliability index based upon a single data collection. But the ultimate reference should go beyond just one testing occasion to other such occasions.

Uses of self-assessment

Self-evaluations

Self-evaluations let students synthesize their past work over a given time period and do reflective writing. Self-evaluations are occasions for reflection and feedback. The goal is not right or wrong answers but thoughtful tentative responses to questions. There are different types of self-evaluations including those which ask students to look back and assess their own work, questions which ask students to make connections over the entire term and questions which ask students to look ahead at future tasks. Self-evaluations can be a series of final entries in their journals as well as short or more extensive assignments that are both in and out of class.

Journals

Journals let students write an ongoing record of thoughts, ideas, experiences and reflections on a given topic. They go beyond the demands of usual written assignments as they promote integration of personal thoughts and expression with materials for a class. Journals provide a systematic means of collecting evidence and documenting learning for self-evaluation and reflections. Journals can be structured or free-form. Structured journals are when students are given specific questions, set of guidelines or target to base their writing. Free-form lets students record thoughts and feelings with little direction. Whatever the form, journals are valuable in assessing a student's ability to observe, challenge, doubt, question, explore and solve problems.

Using journals for assessments require setting certain guidelines. Such guidelines that are helpful include:

- Designing journals to reflect specific learning objectives or goals of the course.
- Adequate instructions are provided to students so they are aware of expectations. To promote effective writing, students should be given specific exercises or guiding questions.
- Discuss explicitly policies about privacy and confidentiality of the information. If journals are to be read or shared with others this should be highlighted. A teacher must disclose and report information that indicates a potential danger or harm.
- Journals should be reviewed periodically and feedback should be provided. Feedback would include constructive remarks, suggestions, questions or encouragement.

Journals can take on many forms. This all depends on the course, class objectives, topic and instructor. The following are ideas that might stimulate instructors in developing their journal assignments based on class needs:

- Observational journal. An observational journal is used to heighten a student's awareness of the relationship between events in the real world and class material. A teacher might want to assign students a specific location for a certain amount of time and then record the observations.
- Personal experience journal. A personal experience journal lets students reflect upon their on experiences in the context of a specific theory or idea. These journals promote active critical processing of course material and active encoding.
- Reading journal. A reading journal is to encourage reading

assignment processing. The journals may target relationships between what a student reads and their experiences.

- Minute reflection journal. These journals can be used in class to promote critical thinking that is related to particular presentations, activities or discussions. Teachers may pose questions then require students to write two or three minutes to record initial thoughts and reactions.
- Listening journals. These journals reflect on a presentation to clarify misconceptions or confusion. Listening journals are best for more difficult subjects. After information is presented, the teacher requires the student to paraphrase and explain what they heard. This can be used to monitor understanding and to clarify any confusion over concepts.
- Expansion journals. These are used to encourage a deep analysis of a particular concept or topic. After instructions, students select a single topic and expand on the information.
- Daily reflection journals. These are used to encourage expression of thoughts, insights and ideas in writing on a habitual basis. These can include emotional and personal thoughts. This can enhance personal insight as well as showing grasps of writing strategies.
- Learning log journal. These journals promote reflection on the learning process and helps in self-assessment of strengths and weaknesses.
- Exchange journal. These journals are used in interactions between two or more peers, utilizing questions and answers.
- Academic journals. These are curriculum-oriented writings that promote reflection on material both before and after instruction. These journals can help teachers focus on issues relevant to student concerns.

Grading student journals can be very subjective due to their personal nature. For fair and consistent grading reflecting assignments, a teacher should have established a set of criteria for evaluation. These criteria should help assist students in preparing journals that are effective in addition to helping with grading. The grading system should be reflective of the learning objectives and assignment goals. Rubrics for grading may be either analytical or holistic systems of scoring. In holistic rubrics, students are given overall criteria for assigning a grade based on the complete journal. For instance the criteria for an "A" might include that students have complete entries in the journals, are insightful, well-developed, the appropriate length, focus on proper objectives and use proper grammar, punctuation and spelling.

Reading Leadership

Reading difficulties

Reading problems

Students who have a reading disorder have problems with their reading skills. Their skills are significantly below that which is normal for the student's age, intelligence and education. The poor reading skills cause problems with the student's academic success and in other areas of life. Signs associated with reading disorders include poor word recognition in reading, very slow reading or making many mistakes. They may also show poor comprehension. Students who suffer from reading disorders normally have low self-esteem, social problems and a higher drop-out rate at school. Reading disorders may be associated with conduct disorder, attention deficit disorder, depression or other learning disorders. Reading disorders are usually brought to the attention of a child's parents in kindergarten or first grade when reading instruction becomes a very important facet of teaching.

Some primary organic conditions are associated with developing learning problems as secondary symptoms. The child's reading and more general learning are thought to result from cognitive or sensory limitation that follow from the diagnosis. These include:

- Cognitive deficiencies. Children with severe cognitive deficiencies usually develop very low, if any, reading achievement. Factors associated with this include very low birth weight, fetal alcohol syndrome, lead poisoning or nutritional deficiencies.
- Hearing impairment is another condition associated with reading difficulty. This may be caused by chronic ear infections that lead to hearing loss.
- Early language impairment. Some children are so clearly behind by age 3 that it arouses concerns of parents, neighbors, preschool teachers or others. Delayed language development is often the first indication of a broader primary condition including developmental disability, autism, or hearing impairment.
- Those with reading problems often have attention deficits.

Research on reading problems suggests that children whose parents or older siblings have shown reading problems are at greater risk for reading difficulties than those children of otherwise similar backgrounds. Factors identified as family risk factors include family history of reading problems, home literacy environment, verbal interaction, language other than English, nonstandard dialect and family-based socioeconomic status. Family patterns of reading problems can be attributed to factors that are either shared genetically or those shared environmentally. Most studies of familial incidence diagnose a child with a reading disability using a severity criterion that would identify between 5 to 10 percent of children who have normal intelligence and have had for what most children is an education that is effective.

The foundations of good reading for children are all the same. All readers need to develop fluency, comprehension and motivation to read in order to become readers who are successful. This is true regardless of the reader's age, aptitude or gender. Children who have reading difficulties are no different. They must also develop the basic foundations for reading and they also require the same type of learning experiences in order for that to happen. Most young children with reading difficulties have problems with development of fluency. The rate at which they read is slow, their word identification is hesitant and they over rely on contextual clues. Since most of their mental or cognitive effort is spent trying to identify words, their comprehension falters.

Eye coordination problems

Two general types of eye coordination problems can affect a young reader -- astigmatism, eye-hand coordination, visual motor problems and other conditions, and esophoria. Children will get into postures that are distorted while trying to get one eye to function. They will often put their head down on their arms; they will cover an eye with their hand or rotate their head so their nose bridge interferes with one eye's vision. Esophoria is another eye coordination problem that tends to turn eyes inward. A child will see objects smaller than they really are. The only way that a child can make the object bigger is to get it closer to him or her.

Discrepancy criteria

Most state and federal guidelines for identifying those with reading disabilities have as a foundation an ability-achievement discrepancy. It is usually operationalized as an IQ-achievement discrepancy. An assumption behind such guidelines has been that poor readers with discrepancies, or the reading disabled, have a unique type of poor reading that is different from other poor reading types. Such criteria have been attacked by reading disability researchers. Research shows that there are many similarities between those who read poorly who have discrepancies and poor readers who have no discrepancies such as children whose IQs are on level with their reading achievement but is not

low enough for them to become retarded. Both groups seem to have problems with word decoding and phonological functions. Yet little evidence is there to support the notion that poor readers with discrepancies can eventually do better than those children with no discrepancies.

Processing tests

An educational diagnosis of reading disorders normally uses processing tests. These are tests of visual processing, memory, language ability and auditory processing. Poor readers do have certain difficulties in certain processing measures such as decoding words and phonological processing. These tests can provide early identification of reading problems and also help plan an educational program for the student. The problem is that word decoding and phonological processing measures are not always emphasized in identification of reading disabilities in schools. Many such measures lack validity and reliability. An interpretation of these tests also presents problems. A poor performance on these tests usually is interpreted as evidence of a processing disorder intrinsic to the reader. But researchers emphasize processing is shaped not only by innate characteristics such as genetics but also experiences such as reading in class.

Problems with assuming biological causes

A frequently used definition of a reading disorder is presumed to be a dysfunction of the central nervous system, or a biological defect. But the actual role of biology is more complex than such an assumption makes. Biological differences can play some role with reading disabilities and in learning to read as they do for a variety of cognitive abilities in humans. But little evidence exists that most children identified in school as reading disabled actually have a biologically-based problem. Evidence also is lacking that factors such as genetics actually keep children from learning to read. Evidence does exist that labeling poor readers and assuming they have an intrinsic disorder caused by biology may create lower teacher expectations.

Unexpected failure

Reading disorders have been looked at as unexpected or unexplained reading failures in contrast to failure from low intelligence, poor listening comprehension, poverty or sensory impairment. Such a concept came about at a time when significantly less was known about the cognitive processes used in learning to read. It is now known that learning to read uses many different abilities and not all correlate with IQ. Someone may have serious problems with word decoding yet still score high in IQ testing. Reading problems are not unexpected for children if there is monitoring of their cognitive abilities such as phonological awareness. The idea of unexpected failure is not useful anymore in conceptualizing problems with reading.

Dyslexia

Typical symptoms of dyslexia include the terms "dysphonetic" and "dyseidetic." A person who is dysphonetic has problems connecting sounds to symbols and may have difficulty sounding out words. Spelling mistakes would show a very poor phonics understanding. This also sometimes known as "auditory" dyslexia because of its relation to the way a person processes language sounds. On the other hand, a dyseidetic person usually understands phonics concepts but has great problems with word recognition and spelling. This is also known as "surface dyslexia" or "visual dyslexia." Words are usually spelled in a way that

can easily be deciphered phonetically but may be far from being right. One might also see transpositions and reversals in spelling but the letters that correspond to the right sounds are there. Most remedial programs use phonics.

Dyslexia involves a brain difference that is not a defect but does make it excessively hard to learn language. A child with dyslexia will have problems from the very beginning in learning to understand speech and being understood. The child might need describe what he or she wants, and might have trouble sequencing words so they are twisted or speak words in an order that is wrong. Children may have problems positioning letters when he or she enters school. It is difficult to recognize because many of its manifestations are part of the natural maturing process of young children. When children get stuck in these stages and it lasts abnormally for a long period that parent and teachers should recognize a possible problem. But a dyslexic mind may have exceptional musical ability for singing or playing an instrument at an age that is early.

Some "red flag" behaviors that may indicate dyslexia include:
- Avoiding difficult tasks, especially those that involve reading, writing or spelling.
- Spending entirely too much time on tasks or not completing work.
- Propping up their head when writing.
- Guessing when he or she does not know a word.
- Knowing a word one day but not remembering it the next day.
- Mixing manuscript with cursive letters.
- Having a vocabulary that exceeds their reading ability.

- Conceptually understanding math but having difficulty reading and writing problems.
- Having a wide spread between verbal and performance scores on standardized tests.
- Demanding excessive attention or acting inappropriately.

Language disorders

The following is a list and descriptions of language disorders:
- Stuttering - an interruption in the rhythm or flow of speech that is characterized by hesitations, repetitions or prolongation of sounds, syllables, words or phrases.
- Articulation disorders - difficulties with the way sounds are formed and put together. They usually are characterized by substituting one sound for an other (wabbit for rabbit), omitting a sound (han for hand) or distorting sounds.
- Voice disorders - characterized by pitches that are inappropriate such as being too high, too low, never changing or breaking, loudness or not loud enough, or quality such as harsh, hoarse, nasal or breathy voices.
- Aphasia - the loss of speech and language abilities as a result of a head injury of a stroke.
- Delayed language - characterized by a marked slowness in vocabulary development and grammar that is needed to express and understand ideas and thoughts.

Traumatic brain injury

Traumatic brain injury may be of the following types:
- Closed head injury, or bruising. This is common at the point of impact and the opposite side of the brain. It is also common where the brain is adjacent to the rough and bony surfaces of the skull.
- Shearing. It is commonly seen in the brain stem from severe head injury and is commonly in the frontal and temporal lobes where the brain surface rubs against bony skull ridges.
- Hematoma, or bleeding. This occurs in areas that receive the brunt of the injury. These injuries are associated with specific deficits that are related to a particular brain area.
- Frontal lobe damage. Deficits in regulating behavior including social and cognitive behavior.

Traumatic brain injury causes the following results:
- Difficulty concentrating.
- Weak orientation to task and difficulties in shifting from task to task.
- Relatively slow performance.
- Difficulty organizing tasks or information.
- Difficulty with abstract thinking.
- Difficulty thinking strategically.
- Difficulty remembering new information or assignments.
- Academic performance lower than it was before the injury.
- Poor awareness of cognitive limitations.
- Impulsive or inappropriate behavior in class.
- Conflicts with teachers or peers.
- Excessive moodiness.
- Exaggerated responses to stress.
- Excessive tiredness.
- Depression and withdrawal.
- Limited safety judgment.
- Anxiety.
- Anger and acting out.
- Apathy.

- Difficulty starting tasks without being prompted to do so.

Accelerating reading achievement

There are times when performance of student achievement may be below par when reflected on state standardized tests. When that happens, taking a focus look at what areas need helps is a good place to start. Even if achievement is lagging overall reading could be a good place to start because it is the prime academic skill. Armed with a starting point, reading teachers and reading specialists can join forces with core academic content area teachers of the selected students. Establish regular lines of communication with the reading teacher and specialist and the content area teachers can be a significant factor in improving problem areas. The content teachers can communicate how students are doing on specific assignments as well as their overall progress, effort, attitude and achievement. Actions can then be focused on the individual student and improvement can occur.

Professional practices related to students and others

Black-white achievement gap

The black-white achievement gap refers to a general difficulty African-American students experience with academic achievement. They consistently perform below non-minority peers in reading, science and mathematics. The gap has had negative economic and social effects. Some studies have suggested the difference may be caused by cultural linguistic or cultural differences. Good language skills are necessary for reading. Vocabulary skills support reading development in both younger and older readers. African-American children have

been shown to have receptive and expressive skills in vocabularies that are below those of their age levels. But vocabulary breadth can be increased by direct teaching methods. Such teaching methods may act as a start in improving reading for young African-American children and may hopefully narrow the so-called gap.

Immigrant students

American schools have been a major agent for helping those children and youth who recently arrived in this country with adapting to the civic and social demands of their new homes. Classroom lessons and socialization on the school yard takes place. But sometimes the home culture teachings and expectations are contrasted with those of American schools. This can lead to labeling children as disabled when none actually exists. These students do have issues with psychosocial stress as they attempt to adapt. A transition that is successful to one's new country requires a secure cross-cultural identity. How much of each culture forms this identity depends on the person's needs, skills, experience, education and support. Recognition of these transitioning needs and support are among the strategic help that can be given to these children.

Immigrant students are often under a great deal of anxiety and stress as they learn English and cope with new surroundings. The pressure can result in feelings of being overwhelmed, confused or frustrated. If this is so, support services such as counselors or social workers may be needed to help relieve this stress. At other times, the way a student responds to a perplexing situation may be misinterpreted by educators. Humans tend to use behaviors that have worked for them before. And students are likely to use behaviors reinforced by the home and home culture. These misunderstandings have sometimes resulted in immigrant children being labeled as emotionally disturbed and are placed in special programs.

It is common for some teachers to become frustrated when they see themselves as unable to reach one or more of their students. Becoming more culturally informed can help enhance the teaching repertoire. The information can also help teachers realize that these students may have trouble under the teaching of any skilled instructor. But the belief that is expressed in a student helps to create persistence and motivation on their part. Linguistic achievements as well as academic ones in the United States are often because of the patience, tolerance and encouragement that American teachers display. Effort is promoted by teachers who are supportive and who create a valuing, welcoming and accepting educational setting.

Schools can help recent immigrants feel welcome and supported while developing positive identities that are cross-cultural. Schools have many ways to assist their student in learning the curriculum and adapting to the American ways. A recent arrival can be partnered with another student who speaks his or her language or dialect, even if they are not from the home region or heritage of the new student. Cross-age tutoring is also an option that might be considered. Perhaps the tutor could be someone from that culture or region of the world, someone who is a recent immigrant as well, or who is an accepting and helpful American youngster. Hiring paraprofessionals who speak the student's language can also be helpful.

Students need to feel welcomed and valued by their teacher. A direct verbal communication may not be feasible but there are other methods of showing acceptance and personal warmth toward students. This will help relieve anxiety and can promote an enthusiasm to learn academics and American patterns of behavior. Smiles are a good way to reach different cultural, ethnic and linguistic groups. Also, teachers should take time to talk with the youngster, even through an interpreter. Having students talk about their prior life will help the teacher become more familiar with their concerns and will also help in emotionally supporting the new student. The teacher may also answer questions about schools and what is needed to live here in America. The teacher may also how he or she can help make the transition easier.

Hispanic culture elementary reading lesson

Children can find places on the map of the United States with names that come from the Spanish language such as San Francisco, Los Angeles, and Pueblo. An activity can be done that invites students to use the library, class or Internet to find Hispanic Americans in history. Students can be invited to design a postage stamp of the Hispanic Heritage stamp series that might show a famous Hispanic American or some aspect of the Hispanic-American culture or history. Students can be given a list of Spanish words and be invited to find the English equivalent such as "ensalada" -- "salad." Invite students to create books to help them learn the Spanish words for the numbers one to 10 and for the common colors. For example, 1 -- uno, yellow -- amarillo.

Culture capsule

A culture capsule is a biliteracy activity that is usually prepared outside class by students but presented during class for about five or 10 minutes. It contains of a paragraph or two and explains one minimal difference between an American custom and that of another culture's custom. It also includes several photos

- 77 -

and other information that is relevant. These capsules can be used in addition by role playing. Students may act out a part of another culture. Essentially the capsule is a brief description of some aspect of the target culture followed by contrasting information from the students' native language culture. These are done orally with teachers giving a brief talk on the chosen cultural point and then leading a discussion on cultures.

Teaching and learning culture

A framework for teaching and learning culture includes:
- Knowing about getting information. The nature of content and getting information. Facts about the United States and what are important facets of its culture?
- Learning objectives -- demonstrating a mastery of information.
- Techniques and activities -- cultural readings, films, videotapes, cultural artifacts, personal anecdotes.
- Note -- how culture is traditionally taught. Are students given information and are they asked to show that they know it.
- Knowing how to develop behaviors -- knowing about what facts you learned and acting upon them.
- Learning objectives -- demonstrating an ability, a fluency, an expertise, confidence and ease.
- Techniques -- dialogs, role playing, simulations and field experiences.
- Knowing where communicative competence in the language occurs. Students know both what to say and how to do it in an appropriate manner.

The following are goals that should be attained in teaching culture:
- Interest. The student shows a curiosity about the target culture and also shows empathy toward its people.
- Who. The student understands that effective communication requires the discovery of the culturally conditioned images that are seen in the minds of people when they think, act and react to the world that is around them.
- When and where. The student recognizes that situational variables and convention mold behavior in significant manners. He or she should know how people in the target culture act in both normal situations and crisis situations.
- Why. The student knows that people generally act how the do because they are using options for satisfying basic physical and psychological needs and that cultural patterns are interrelated and tend mutually to support the satisfactions of needs.

Students learning culture should react appropriately in social situations. They should describe a pattern in the culture. They should recognize a pattern when it is illustrated. They should be able to explain patterns. They should predict how a pattern is likely to apply in a given situation. They should describe or manifest an attitude that is important for making oneself acceptable in a foreign society. They should evaluate the form of a statement concerning a culture pattern. They should describe or demonstrate defensible methods of analyzing a sociocultural whole. They should identify basic human purposes that make significant that what being taught is understood. There are other steps that can be made with similar goals.

Ways to measure the change in attitudes about foreign cultures include:

- Social distance scales. This is to measure the degree to which one separates oneself socially from members of another culture. For instance: Would you marry, have someone as a close friend, have as an acquaintance, work with or have as a close friend?
- Semantic differential scales. This is to judge the defined culture group in terms of a number of traits that are bipolar. For instance, are people from this culture clean, are they dirty, are they good, are they bad?
- Statements. This is to put a check in front of statements the student agrees with. Is the person you know envious of others, self-indulgent, quick to understand, tactless?
- Self-esteem change. This is to measure self-esteem changes in the primary grades. For instance, am I happy with myself?

Students may display behaviors in their cultures but are different that those in the American mainstream thus they are at risk for being labeled by uniformed educators as having behaviors that are "wrong." Teachers should familiarize themselves with a student's home culture's values and practices. There should be an awareness of differences that promote understanding and tolerance, acceptance, celebration of others and their ways and acceptance. Information on other cultures can be found in many textbooks, travel books and on various Web sites. Another way to develop familiarity with a student's cultural background is the use of a "cultural informant." This is someone who might be familiar with the group and their ways such as teachers or other successful members of that cultural group.

Obstacles a reading specialist faces

Reading specialists know that a viable reading program takes in the needs and learning styles of all students. But in reality there are a number of obstacles in making this happen. There may be a lack of money or personnel. Education also operates under a system of mandates, theories, strategies and trends that are fragmented. Reading series or manuals may attempt to bring some kid of consistency to a district or building. Sometimes they are used and sometimes they are not. In districts that are ideal, the need for reading specialists is not in large numbers. The districts that have little financial resources need reading specialists more than can generally be afforded.

Classroom teachers have recognized there is a problem in ensuring that those who need a reading specialist receive the help they need. Those children needing help may have failed in the mainstream environment and need ways to match their strengths and needs. It should be recognized that children may not always seem enthusiastic about reading but despite what they do to mask it, they really want to learn how to read. The specialist can work with the classroom teacher so that he or she will take ownership of these children who need help. Working with the classroom teacher will bring extra benefits to the student and the classroom. Both classroom teacher and reading specialist can work together to provide what the student needs, find out the student's achievements or lack of it and then work to modify the instruction if need be so the child will learn to read.

Assessing reading strengths and weaknesses

A number of tests are available online on the Internet for assessing comprehension levels and there also are paper and pencil charts for assessing fluency orally. Likewise, there are tests that determine the understanding of affixes, prefixes, suffixes, compounds and contractions to name a few. The biggest problem is deciding which test to use in obtaining a snapshot of the child's ability to read and comprehend. The reading specialist and classroom teacher can work together to administer these tests to develop a plan of action to help at-risk students. These tests may be formal or standardized. They may either be norm-referenced or criterion-referenced. Good classroom teachers and reading specialists will blend the results of these tests to come up with an instructional model for the student.

Communicating reading evaluations with parents

Parents of children who have been assessed as having problems with reading should be told the various steps necessary for an accurate and fair determination. The first step is using what is already known. A group of people – reading specialist, teacher --evaluates the child with information that is already available. If more information is needed, then the second step is collecting more information. The school will ask the parent for permission to evaluate the child. The school then collects more information. The third step is deciding whether the child is eligible for special education or related services. Those who are doing the evaluation then come to the parents to decide. The fourth step is developing the child's educational program. If the child is eligible for special education a program to meet the child's need will be developed.

Parents whose children are being tested for reading problems should be assured by teachers or reading specialists that the evaluation:

- Uses the native language such as Spanish or sign language unless it clearly is impossible to do so.
- Does not discriminate against the child because he or she has some type of disability or comes from a background that is racially or culturally different.
- Must use evaluators who know how to give the tests they decide to use.
- Results will be used to decide if the child has a disability and to determine the educational program needs for the child. These decisions cannot be based solely on one evaluation.

Communicating with a family about their child's reading development can be a challenge especially if it is an exceptional child with culturally-diverse parents. Those who provide services to those of different cultural backgrounds should be aware of unique perspectives or communications styles that are common to those cultures. It is not always to tell how parents are reacting when they are told their child has a disability because of the different ways people deal with feelings such as anxiety, anger, disappointment and embarrassment. It is especially important for parents who have been outside of the mainstream of education in the United States to be made known of the educational choices that are available to the child. To do this, professionals should be sensitive to different values and experiences as well as beliefs that may be held by various ethnic and cultural groups toward special education.

In explaining the reading development of a child from a culturally diverse background, educators should use sensitivity by sending messages home to the parents in their native language, using an appropriate reading level and listen to the messages that are returned. Courtesy, sincerity and ample opportunity and time show concerns that can promote communications with and participation by parents who come from backgrounds that are culturally different. It is important during meetings that an ample opportunity is available for the parent to respond at meetings without interruption. If a parent is formulating a response and has not expressed it quickly, this should not be viewed as the parent being uninterested. Educators should listen with empathy and realize that parents can change feelings of trust to skepticism or curiosity as the understanding of programs and policies increase.

Educators who deal with families of different cultural group when communicating about their children's reading progress should carefully consider these observations:

- Sharing space. People from different cultures use, value and share space differently. It is considered appropriate for people to stand very close to each other while talking in some cultures whereas others like to keep farther apart. For instance, Hispanics often view Americans as distant because they prefer more space.
- Touching. Rules for touching differ from culture to culture. In Hispanic and other Latin cultures there is often more touching seen when talking and individuals usually embrace when greeting each other. It is not customary in Vietnamese or other Asian cultures to shake hands with those of the opposite sex.
- Eye contact. It is customary to avert eyes among African-Americans while Anglo Americans prefer to make direct eye contact.

Performance factors

Teachers may look for specific performance factors that can be passed along to the reading or other specialists for assessment to decide if a child needs modified reading instruction. These factors are:

- Continuous improvement. Is the student doing better than before? Is the student doing better than in earlier grades?
- Comparative performance. Do the results show that the student is doing well in comparison to children in comparable settings?
- Absolute performance. Do the results show the student is reaching the school's desired level of performance?
- Small-group performance. Do the results show that children of a similar group as the student (limited English, Title I students) are making better progress that that of the student?

Promoting professional growth

Conjoint behavioral consultation

Conjoint behavioral consultation (CBC) is a partnership model of service delivery in which parents, educators, other primary caregivers and service providers all work in collaboration to meet the developmental needs of children, address their concerns and to achieve success by promoting the competencies of all parties concerned. CBC creates an opportunity for families and schools to work together for a common interest and to build upon and promote the capabilities and strengths of the family members and school personnel. Individual needs are identified and acted upon using an organized approach that is data-based and that has mutual and collaborative interactions between parents and children along with guidance and assistance of consultants such as school psychologists.

Conjoint behavioral consultant partnerships (CBC) can be implemented through four stages: needs identification, needs analysis, plan development and plan evaluation. Three of these stages use interviews to structure the decisions to be made. Overall, the goal is to effectively address needs and desires of parents and teachers for children. Specific objectives include:

- Addressing concerns as they happen across rather than only within settings.
- Enhancing home-school partnerships to helps student learning and performance.
- Establishing joint responsibility for solving problems.
- Improving communications between children, family and school personnel.
- Assessing needs in a comprehensive and functional way.
- Promoting continuity and consistency among agents of change and across various settings.
- Providing opportunities for powers to become empowered using strength-based orientation.

Reading First Program

The Reading First Program is a federal initiative adopted by the states and school districts with a goal of ensuring all children in the United States learn to read by the end of the third grade. The Reading First program will help states and districts apply some of the scientifically-based research on successful reading instruction as well as the instructional

and assessment tools consistent with the research to teach all children to read. These assessment tools include progress monitoring. The program will help provide necessary aid to states and districts by establishing research-based reading programs for children in kindergarten through the third grade. Funds for the program also focus on providing increased teacher professional development to ensure all teachers have the skills they need to effectively teach this program.

Training in the five essential components of reading instruction is one of the most important elements of a quality professional development plan under the Reading First initiative. Teachers should learn effective strategies for providing explicit and systematic instruction for each component. Those components are:

- Phonemic awareness. Teachers should understand the difference between phonemic awareness and phonics. Phonemic awareness focuses on hearing sounds and learning how those sounds are put together.
- Phonics. Teachers should be trained in explicit and systematic phonics instruction based on scientifically based reading research.
- Fluency. Teachers will learn the various techniques for reading fluency such as teacher modeling, repeating reading aloud and choral reading.
- Reading vocabulary. Teachers can learn several effective techniques for teaching vocabulary.
- Reading comprehension. Professional development can give teachers certain comprehension strategies that can help students understand what they read.

There are certain requirements for implementing federal Reading First professional development plans. They include:

- The plans must closely align with the principles of scientifically-based reading research and the five essential components of reading instruction. The programs must provide instruction in scientifically-based reading instructional materials, programs, strategies and approaches. Also, the programs must train teachers in the appropriate use of assessment tools and analysis and interpretation of gathered data.
- An eligible professional development provider must deliver the professional development program. To be eligible, the provider must be able to train teachers, including special education teachers, in reading instruction that is grounded in scientifically-based reading research.
- Teachers must be instructed in teaching all components of reading instruction and must understand how the components are related, the progression in which they should be taught and the underlying structure of the English language.

Since Reading First is a federal initiative, many states may have similar state guidelines for carrying out the initiative such as summer reading programs. Some guideline examples might include:

- The use of Reading First-approved core, supplemental and intervention programs.
- Daily 90-minute uninterrupted reading instructional blocks. This would include systematic delivery of explicit instruction using approved core reading program material.

- Intervention services provided for students who are below the mastery of reading skills.
- Evidence of teacher's use of data to drive instruction. Reports on the program developed by the state will include information on the number of students served, the summer school teacher credentials, student achievement gain and percentage of students meeting end of grade benchmarks at beginning and end of the summer program.

Certain leadership guidelines are needed for educators implementing Reading First programs. Included in such guidelines are:

- Providing a vision. Implementing such a program requires a clear vision how students and teacher will benefit from a new approach to reading. Teachers can understand that they can make a greater impact on many students' reading skills because they are better able to diagnose reading problems.
- Set priorities. The name Reading First Initiative is so named because reading is critical to the future success of students in a number of content areas.
- Create ownership. Programs can run more efficiently when teachers help in decision-making.
- Foster peer support. Teachers should have the time to meet with reading specialists and other colleagues for formal professional development as well as informal opportunities to talk.

Reading specialist as a resource

Reading specialists help staff develop knowledge of literacy theory and instructions. They are consultants and collaborating teachers for classroom teachers, aides, parents and other teachers such as special education, speech, music and art. Some schools have chosen to replace reading specialists with teaching assistants who lack specialized literacy training. When this happens, a grave injustice is done to students, teachers and the literacy program. Reading specialists provide expert instruction to learners who differ in language, learning style, culture and ability; they share effective learning strategies and practices with school staff and parents; and they serve as an expert of sorts for the school and district on information about reading and literacy instruction.

Promoting colleague collaboration

The reading specialist in a school setting provides a wide variety of services, many of which are in a collaborative effort with colleagues. The specialist works with teachers to promote and develop the literacy program as well as developing thinking strategies in the classroom. As a diagnostician, the specialist administers both group and individual evaluations of reading achievement and recommends activities to build comprehension. For intervention, the specialist works with teachers as well as students and small groups for providing instruction and for building competencies in literacy. In addition, the reading specialist works with the staff and parents in order to promote various events to gather support for the literacy program and that support literacy as a whole.

Professional development

Classroom teachers feel the stress of student achievement and even worry about job security what with the pressures of high-stakes testing and other factors that can be frustrating. Educators think of themselves as professionals but a

professional attitude is not always fostered by school leaders. These leaders should create and advance a climate that allow teachers access to cutting-edged, research-based professional development in reading programs to help encourage them to share instructional methods and strategies. Ways that help districts start professional development must develop or find programs that:

- Provide a strong correlation to district and school goals.
- Be based on scientifically-based reading research.
- Include a format that provides ongoing training.
- Offer frequent opportunities for teacher dialogue and sharing as part of the process.

Communities

Schools are opening their doors more and more for community resources to help serve students and family. So-called "full-service" schools show that schools are paying attention to their holistic as well as academic needs. These schools offer health, counseling, social service, after school and other programs to help support learning and growth. Some community-initiated activities are also transforming schools. These communities are taking responsibility to use information about schools to help offer new ways of looking at improving schools. They are working with schools on recurring problems. The schools are beginning to change in ways that bring more voices to the table when it comes to decision-making.

Schools that actively develop students' critical thinking skills and real-world knowledge applications as well as services and enrichment activities should forge new relationships with communities in order to improve learning for the school's students. This helps community member to get to know the school and its staff better. It also structures the school to meet some broader needs that the families of students might have. The school can also become a resource for families and community members. The school can serve as a center for community meetings, local theatrical productions, candidate nights, health screening or other activities that help the community. Forging these good relationships can help the school in a number of ways such as when school bond elections roll around and require the community as voters.

There are a number of concrete steps that community members can take to help schools improve and especially to help more children to read. Community members can:

- Become a learning partner or tutor. The citizen can tutor a child in his or here neighborhood or in a local elementary school. Volunteers might read with or to a child for 30 minutes a week, at least eight weeks and can take the child to the library to him or her a library card.
- Volunteer to serve as a community coordinator for a community reading program. A number of organizations can work to recruit tutors. This person can also work with local schools to match community members and children.
- Ask organizations to help support community reading programs. Local businesses can be encouraged to donate supplies or allow employees time off to volunteer in school.

Professional development programs

Reading program guidelines

A school district might implement reading program guidelines that include the following:

- Each student in the district has the right to learn to read regardless of race, creed, color, gender, or social or economic status.
- Reading is not just a curriculum subject. Reading is a developmental process which involves language, emotions, thinking, interaction, and judgments. Reading permeates the entire curriculum at every grade level.
- Reading requires skills which can and should be taught at appropriate times in appropriate ways.
- The district will provide educational programs and developmental reading instruction for grades K-12 that will assure every student at every grade level has the opportunity to acquire reading skills.

Monitoring school wide reading programs

Critically looking at goals and needs school wide programs should recognize that the ultimate goal is better results. Measuring progress, being accountable for results and making changes based on reliable data are vital aspects of school wide improvement. Many school leaders look upon this process as a work in progress. Continuous data-driven accountability involves teams such as teachers and reading specialists to engage in the following:

- Combine information from multiple measurements on all groups of students.
- Organize data to clarify strengths and needs of the school as a whole.
- Disaggregate information on students to determine whether some subgroups are experiencing common problems.
- Keep alert to the implications for the quality of education supported by the school as a whole.

Data sources can be used to critically analyze school wide programs such as reading so that appropriate changes can be made to meet students' goals and needs. Many schools have linked aligned instructional benchmarks to broader objectives that are periodically measured by their state's assessment programs. Schools, through aligned assessments, can examine results for several purposes to track absolute progress, compare against benchmark goals and to find patters that reveal progress or weaknesses over time. An ongoing analysis of data can determine adjustments that are timely. Aligned information can let educators examine instructional variations that might make a difference in academic achievements. This lets educators ask: What should be done at various levels within the classroom or school wide to prevent problems the data identifies.

Monitoring a school literacy program involves systematically examining students' reading progress and teachers' instructional strategies. Monitoring is a continuous process. Any monitoring has three basic components: collecting information regularly, analyzing and evaluating that information and taking action to improve student performance. Other activities may precede these components such as articulating questions on which to focus the

monitoring and determining gaps in practice. When teachers monitor the school's literacy program, they keep tabs on student achievement and success in reading and writing. They collect literacy-focused assessment data including standardized tests and alternative assessments. They also look beyond assessment data to children's attitudes toward reading, comments from families and other pertinent information.

Before monitoring literacy programs can get started teachers and administrators should be aware of some concerns about monitoring. Attempts to evaluate reading programs and student reading achievement often confuses the issue instead of making it clearer. Reasons for the confusion include the fact that the evaluation is often initiated as an afterthought. A plan is not in place to answer initial evaluation questions before the process of teaching reading starts in classrooms. Secondly, the evaluation may be hampered by unclear objectives. If little attention has been spent on why the evaluation is taking place, what is being evaluated may not be clear. There is also confusion about the term evaluation. Evaluation determines the worth of something. Evaluation systems are based on data and assessment information. Continuous progress monitoring in order to critically analyze school programs such as reading is an ongoing strategy with multiple measurements. Useful information requires assessments often, at least four times a year. Measurement strategies include qualitative methods such as personal interviews and focus groups along with standardized tests and surveys. These provide in-depth information about the results of reforms. No single survey or all-purpose data collection tool will meet a school's needs for information. Multiple measurements are vital in tracking the process of change. Data systems should not be relied upon for monitoring all things. When making a change, teachers rely on both hard data and their intuition. But, those perspectives should be validated by assessments from the outside.

Continuous monitoring that allows analysis of school wide programs such as reading gives the faculty and staff a sense of ownership by putting accountability in their hands. Few surprises exist in continuous monitoring because the school is in control of its own assessment. Teachers and school leaders score many of their own tests so they learn the results immediately. As teams such as reading specialists and classroom teachers look at the data they look for information about different aspects of the subject within the school. With data analysis questions may be asked such as: Are there grades with an especially strong or weak showing in the subject? Are non-English or limited-English speakers improving the use of their test materials?

Monitoring a school's literacy program is of critical importance but some teachers faced with the day-to-day workload of preparing lessons, instructing, keeping records, disciplining and correcting papers may consider the monitoring something for which they do not have time. The principal or superintendent should emphasize the importance of monitoring the literacy program and ensure teachers have adequate time for data collection and interpreting. Some educators may suggest the use of data already available rather than collecting new data. In such situations, the questions for monitoring can be manipulated to focus only on data that is readily available. However, this will yield reliable and valid results and will not be as helpful in improving student learning goals.

Student peer training

Students have long had informal, untrained peer helping networks. Students share their concerns with each other naturally while at lunch, after school and while talking on the phone at home. The seriousness of the problems discussed has changed somewhat in today's world. Students may likely know someone who was pregnant or suicidal, who had a drug problem, was being abused or who had an eating disorder. But many of these students with such problems do not seek adult help for their problems. This results in a crisis where a student's coping mechanisms are not effective and many students end up getting little or no help from professionals. Peer programs offer the ability to increase the student's skill in responding and helping friends, and train students to know when there is a crisis and where the peer may be referred.

The peer helper and adult resource connection is not often understood by educators who are unfamiliar with the concept. But that linkage is a bedrock of the program. Young people with serious worries can be helped by their peers and adults. Help can come early and can take place where there is trust. Students can build a circle of support around them with such programs. It is a challenge, however, because students do feel rejected or neglected by their peers. Research shows that the best way to keep stress away is being part of a stable, tight-knit group. Peer helpers can be trained to help with continued needs that help foster more well-rounded communities within schools.

Intended outcomes for peer helpers include:

- The helpers being more likely to refer their friends to adults for help when there is a need.

- The helpers will know when, where and how to make referrals to the right resource people.
- An increased understanding of the seriousness of depression can be gained by the peer helpers and they can help identify the mixed behavior types that can be warning signs of depression.
- The helpers can identify and respond to warning signs of suicide.
- Peer helpers can develop an increased opportunity to improve the quality of a school's circle of support.
- Peer helpers show an increased level of personal development such as the sense of personal efficacy, self-esteem, social responsibility and locus of control.

Conveying high expectations

Researchers have found certain ways that school may let students know the school's expectations of them are high:

- Establishing policies that emphasize how important it is to achieve academically. Parents can be notified if students are not meeting the academic expectations or setting minimally acceptable achievement levels for students to participate in sports or extracurricular activities.
- Use slogans that communicate high expectations for the students such as "Yes we can."
- Protect instructional time and discourage tardiness, absenteeism and interruptions.
- Provide insistent coaching to students who experience difficulty with learning tasks. Researchers say that excusing children from trying hard to succeed in academics because it is not fair or

hopeless to expect any more, or trying to protect them from failure does not really help students in learning. It detracts from academic skills and can also lower motivation and self-esteem.

Curriculum development

Curriculum-based assessment

Instructional strategies are not fail-proof when it comes to teaching students new skills. But there are a number of data-based strategies that have been identified that when used with an objective and systematic assessment can lead to a curriculum that will help improve student performance. Such an assessment is curriculum-based assessment. These are models of assessment that emphasize a direct relationship to the student's curriculum. These assessments use measures from the curriculum to evaluate the effectiveness of instruction and what changes to the instruction can lead to more effective teaching methods and improved student achievement. The assessment provides information on how the student's behavior changes on a generic task of constant difficulty. Increases in the behavior being measured on equivalent forms of the task would represent growth academically.

A problem-solving process can be used with methods to assess or measure how well the curriculum is meeting students' needs so that changes in the curriculum can be made. The process includes:

- Identifying the problem to be solved. For instance, a marked underachievement in reading.
- Identifying alternative solutions to the problem such as a new reading method.

- Implement new programs and test alternative solutions. Revise unsuccessful solutions.
- Terminate the problem. This includes revising unsuccessful instructional programs. When making changes in a student's instructional program, teachers should be aware of various characteristics of instruction that can be changed that are under the direct control of the teacher.

Evolutionary and revolutionary changes in instruction

Instructional changes can be viewed as revolutionary or evolutionary. Revolutionary are those changes with major modifications in an instructional program. Evolutionary changes are minor ones. Evolutionary changes may be made in certain parts of the instructional plan such as time, activity, materials or motivation. A revolutionary change could include the method of instruction from a language experience approach to direct instruction. Technically sound achievement indicators for such decisions include the number of words read correctly for reading, the number of correct letter sequences in two minutes or the number of words spelled in two minutes for spelling. For written expression the indicators could be the number of words written in two minutes, the number of correctly spelled words in two minutes or the number of correct word sequences in two minutes.

Effective curricula

Effective curricula that are culturally responsive share certain characteristics. These include:
- The curriculum is integrated and interdisciplinary. It does not rely on one-time activities or "sprinkling" the traditional curriculum with a few minority individuals.
- It is authentic, connected to the child's real life and child-centered. It uses materials from the child's culture and history to illustrate concepts and principles.
- It develops critical thinking skills.
- It often incorporates strategies that use cooperative learning and whole language instruction, self-esteem building and recognizes diverse styles of learning.
- It is supported by appropriate staff development and pre-service preparation.
- It is part of a coordinated strategy. Successful implementation requires a school climate that is receptive and recognition that the hidden curriculum in any school can be a powerful ally or a powerful enemy.

Cultural relevance

A number of criteria should be evaluated when looking for curriculum materials that are culturally relevant. Teachers should look for invisibility, stereotyping, selectivity, imbalance, unreality, isolation, language bias and fragmentation. Also to be looked for in books is the inappropriate treatment of African Americans, Native Americans, Asian Americans and Hispanic Americans especially when the "one size fits all view" is expressed. This is where instructional material reflects through generalization that there is a single Hispanic, African, Asian or Native culture. The sidebar approach also should be avoided. This is where a few isolated events relevant to ethnic experiences are relegated to a box or sidebar that is set apart from the rest of the text.

There are commonly differences found between cultures in how one prefers to learn some type of information and how that knowledge is displayed. A lack of understanding of different learning styles and the influence of one's cultural background can bring conflict, lack of achievement and confusion. It is common for a culturally different student's preferred ways of learning to be in contrast with those ways that are used in American schools and are suggested for teacher training programs. It is important to discern the learning preferences for a recently arrived immigrant student and then teach to that style. Evaluation of the learning and teaching styles and process for acquiring a second culture and language may change how students are taught in America. Some studies suggest teachers understanding preferred learning styles of students allows them to adjust their style to maximize teaching.

Teachers should develop learning environments that are reflective of their students' social, cultural and linguistic experiences. They serve as instructors, mediators, guides, consultants and advocates for students in helping them to find a way that is most effective to connect their cultural and community-based knowledge to their learning experiences in the classroom. A key criterion for teaching that is culturally relevant is nurturing and supporting competence in cultures both at school and home. Teachers should use the student's home cultural experience as a base on which to build skills and increase knowledge. Content that is learned this way becomes more significant to the student and helps facilitate a transfer of school learning to real-life.

A teacher can become a facilitator in transferring school knowledge to that of real life by involving a student's home culture in learning. Ways to do this include:

- Have students share artifacts from home that are reflective of their culture.
- Have students write about traditions that their families share.
- Have students research different aspects of their culture.
- Have members of the community who share a culture with your students speak to the class on various subjects.
- Involve the class in making something relevant to other cultures (such as a piñata for studying the Hispanic culture.)

Disseminating research across grade levels

Just as students must perform research at the university level, reading specialists must also do research -- about research. Finding literary research and disseminating it across grade levels may be crucial to success in a reading program. Some tips for finding such research:

- Focus the topic. State the topic as a question and ask other questions that might also address the topic.
- Find overviews or background information. Abstracts of research can give the major aspects of the topic being researched without going into a lot of detail. Abstracts can also be used to find out important facts such as names of people and concepts that can be used as keywords in a search.
- Prepare the search. Circle the main words in the topic statement. Brainstorm for related words that might be used to describe the topic.
- Find books. Books provide detailed information on a topic.

Practice Test

Practice Questions

1. *Sea* and *see*, *fair* and *fare*, are called:
    a. Homophones
    b. Antonyms
    c. Homophobes
    d. Twin words

2. Another name for a persuasive essay is:
    a. Dynamic essay
    b. Convincing essay
    c. Argumentative essay
    d. Position paper

3. A teacher is working with a group of third graders at the same reading level. Her goal is to improve reading fluency. She asks each child in turn to read a page from a book about mammal young. She asks the children to read with expression. She also reminds them they don't need to stop between each word; they should read as quickly as they comfortably can. She cautions them, however, not to read so quickly that they leave out or misread a word. The teacher knows the components of reading fluency are:
    a. Speed, drama, and comprehension
    b. Cohesion, rate, and prosody
    c. Understanding, rate, and prosody
    d. Rate, accuracy, and prosody

4. "Language load" refers to:
    a. The basic vocabulary words a first grader has committed to memory.
    b. The number of unrecognizable words an English Language Learner encounters when reading a passage or listening to a teacher.
    c. The damage that carrying a pile of heavy books could cause to a child's physique.
    d. The number of different languages a person has mastered.

5. A syllable must contain:
    a. A vowel
    b. A consonant
    c. Both a vowel and a consonant
    d. A meaning

6. A third-grade teacher has several students reading above grade level. Most of the remaining students are reading at grade level. There are also a few students reading below grade level. She decides to experiment. Her hypothesis is that by giving the entire class a chapter book above grade level, high-level readers will be satisfied, grade-level readers will be challenged in a positive way, and students reading below grade level will be inspired to improve. Her method is most likely to:
   a. Succeed, producing students reading at an Instructional reading level. High-level readers will be happy to be given material appropriate to their reading level. Grade-level readers will challenge themselves to improve reading strategies in order to master the text. Because only a few of the students are reading below grade level, the other students, who feel happy and energized, will inspire the slower readers by modeling success.
   b. Succeed, producing students reading at an Independent reading level. High-level readers will independently help grade-level readers who will, in turn, independently help those below grade level.
   c. Fail, producing students at a Frustration reading level. Those reading below grade level are likely to give up entirely. Those reading at grade level are likely to get frustrated and form habits that will actually slow down their development.
   d. Fail, producing students reading at a Chaotic reading level. By nature, children are highly competitive. The teacher has not taken into consideration multiple learning styles. The children who are at grade level will either become bitter and angry at those whose reading level is above grade level or simply give up. The children reading below grade level will not be able to keep up and will in all likelihood act out their frustration or completely shut down.

7. Of the three tiers of words, the most important words for direct instruction are:
   a. Tier-one words
   b. Common words
   c. Tier-two words
   d. Words with Latin roots

8. At the beginning of each month, Mr. Yi has Jade read a page or two from a book she hasn't seen before. He notes the total number of words in the section, and also notes the number of times she leaves out or misreads a word. If Jade reads the passage with less than 3% error, Mr. Yi is satisfied that Jade is:
   a. Reading with full comprehension.
   b. Probably bored and should try a more difficult book.
   c. Reading at her Independent reading level.
   d. Comfortable with the syntactical meaning.

9. The purpose of corrective feedback is:
   a. To provide students with methods for explaining to the teacher or classmates what a passage was about.
   b. To correct an error in reading a student has made, specifically clarifying where and how the error was made so that the student can avoid similar errors in the future.
   c. To provide a mental framework that will help the student correctly organize new information.
   d. To remind students that error is essential in order to truly understand and that it is not something to be ashamed of.

10. Dr. Jenks is working with a group of high school students. They are about to read a science book about fossils. Before they begin, she writes the words *stromatolites, fossiliferous,* and *eocene* on the board. She explains the meaning of each word. These words are examples of:
   a. Academic words
   b. Alliteration
   c. Content-specific words
   d. Ionization

11. Which of the following best explains the importance prior knowledge brings to the act of reading?
   a. Prior knowledge is information the student gets through researching a topic prior to reading the text. A student who is well-prepared through such research is better able to decode a text and retain its meaning.
   b. Prior knowledge is knowledge the student brings from previous life or learning experiences to the act of reading. It is not possible for a student to fully comprehend new knowledge without first integrating it with prior knowledge.
   c. Prior knowledge is predictive. It motivates the student to look for contextual clues in the reading and predict what is likely to happen next.
   d. Prior knowledge is not important to any degree to the act of reading, because every text is self-contained and therefore seamless. Prior knowledge is irrelevant in this application.

12. A cloze test evaluates a student's:
   a. Reading fluency.
   b. Understanding of context and vocabulary.
   c. Phonemic skills.
   d. Ability to apply the alphabetic principle to previously unknown material.

13. Sight words are:
   a. Common words with irregular spelling.
   b. Words that can easily be found on educational websites.
   c. Any word that can be seen, including text words, words on signs, brochures, banners, and so forth.
   d. There is no such thing; because oral language is learned before written language, all words are ultimately based on sound. The correct term is sound words and includes all words necessary to decode a particular text.

14. *Phone, they, church.* The underlined letters in these words are examples of:
   a. Consonant blend
   b. Consonant shift
   c. Continental shift
   d. Consonant digraph

15. Phonemic awareness is a type of:
   a. Phonological awareness. Phonemic awareness is the ability to recognize sounds within words.
   b. Phonics. It is a teaching technique whereby readers learn the relationship between letters and sounds.
   c. Alphabetization. Unless a reader knows the alphabet, phonemic awareness is useless.
   d. Syntactical awareness. Understanding the underlying structure of a sentence is key to understanding meaning.

16. All members of a group of kindergarten students early in the year are able to chant the alphabet. The teacher is now teaching the students what the alphabet looks like in written form. The teacher points to a letter and the students vocalize the correspondent sound. Alternatively, the teacher vocalizes a phoneme and a student points to it on the alphabet chart. The teacher is using _____ in her instruction.
   a. Letter–sound correspondence
   b. Rote memorization
   c. Predictive analysis
   d. Segmentation

17. A fourth-grade teacher is preparing her students for a reading test in which a number of words have been replaced with blanks. The test will be multiple-choice; there are three possible answers given for each blank. The teacher instructs the children to read all the possible answers and cross out any answer that obviously doesn't fit. Next, the students should "plug in" the remaining choices and eliminate any that are grammatically incorrect or illogical. Finally, the student should consider contextual clues in order to select the best answer. This in an example of:
   a. Strategy instruction
   b. Diagnostic instruction
   c. Skills instruction
   d. Multiple-choice instruction

18. The term "common words" means:
   a. One-syllable words with fewer than three letters. Some examples are it, an, a, I, go, to, and in. They are the first words an emergent writer learns.
   b. One-syllable words with fewer than five letters. Some examples include sing, goes, sit, rock, walk, and took.
   c. Words that are ordinary or unexceptional; because they tend to flatten a piece of writing, they should be avoided.
   d. Familiar, frequently used words that do not need to be taught beyond primary grades.

19. Which is greater, the number of English phonemes or the number of letters in the alphabet?
   a. The number of letters in the alphabet, because they can be combined to create phonemes.
   b. The number of phonemes. A phoneme is the smallest measure of language sound.
   c. They are identical; each letter "owns" a correspondent sound.
   d. Neither. Phonemes and alphabet letters are completely unrelated.

20. _Train, brain, spring._ The underlined letters are examples of:
   a. Consonant digraph
   b. Consonant blend
   c. Consonant shift
   d. Continental shift

21. It is the beginning of the school year. To determine which second-grade students might need support, the reading teacher wants to identify those who are reading below grade level. She works with students one at a time. She gives each child a book at a second-grade reading level and asks the child to read out loud for two minutes. Children who will need reading support are those who read:
   a. Fewer than 100 words in the time given.
   b. Fewer than 200 words in the time given.
   c. More than 75 words in the time given.
   d. The entire book in the time given.

22. The most effective strategy for decoding sight words is:
   a. Segmenting sight words into syllables. Beginning readers are understandably nervous when encountering a long word that isn't familiar. Blocking off all but a single syllable at a time renders a word manageable and allows the reader a sense of control over the act of reading.
   b. Word families. By grouping the sight word with similar words, patterns emerge.
   c. A phonemic approach. When students understand the connection between individual words and their sounds, they will be able to sound out any sight word they encounter.
   d. None; sight words cannot be decoded. Readers must learn to recognize these words as wholes on sight.

23. The reading teacher is working with a group of English Language Learners. Which of the following strategies will help these students learn to read with enhanced fluency?
   a. The teacher reads aloud while students follow the words in their books.
   b. Tape-assisted reading.
   c. Having the students' parents or another trustworthy adult read with the child each evening for 45 minutes.
   d. A and B.

24. "Decoding" is also called:
   a. Remediation
   b. Deciphering
   c. Alphabetic principle
   d. Deconstruction

25. A reading teacher is working with a group of English Language Learners. She has asked them to study sequentially the pictures in a storybook and then tell her what they think the story is about. This approach will help the students understand the _____ of the story.
   a. Theme
   b. Context
   c. Events
   d. Deeper meaning

26. Phonological awareness activities are:
    a. Oral
    b. Visual
    c. Both A and B
    d. Semantically based

27. A student is able to apply strategies to comprehend the meanings of unfamiliar words; can supply definitions for words with several meanings such as *crucial, criticism,* and *witness*; and is able to reflect on her background knowledge in order to decipher a word's meaning. These features of effective reading belong to which category?
    a. Word recognition
    b. Vocabulary
    c. Content
    d. Comprehension

28. A reading teacher is assessing an eighth grader to determine her reading level. Timed at a minute, the student reads with 93% accuracy. She misreads an average of seven words out of 100. What is her reading level?
    a. She is reading at a Frustration level.
    b. She is reading at an Excellence level.
    c. She is reading at an Instructional level.
    d. She is reading at an Independent level.

29. When should students learn how to decode?
    a. Decoding is the most basic and essential strategy to becoming a successful reader. It should be introduced to kindergartners during the first two weeks of school.
    b. Decoding is not a teachable skill. It is an unconscious act and is natural to all learners.
    c. Decoding should be taught only after children have mastered every letter–sound relationship as well as every consonant digraph and consonant blend. They should also be able to recognize and say the 40 phonemes common to English words and be able to recognize at least a dozen of the most common sight words.
    d. Decoding depends on an understanding of letter–sound relationships. As soon as a child understands enough letters and their correspondent sounds to read a few words, decoding should be introduced.

30. *Since, whether,* and *accordingly* are examples of which type of signal words?
    a. Common, or basic, signal words
    b. Compare/contrast words
    c. Cause–effect words
    d. Temporal sequencing words

31. A class is reading *The Heart Is a Lonely Hunter*. The teacher asks students to write a short paper explaining the story's resolution. She is asking them to locate and discuss the story's:
    a. Outcome
    b. Highest or most dramatic moment
    c. Plot
    d. Lowest point

32. A student encounters a multisyllabic word. She's not sure if she's seen it before. What should she do first? What should she do next?
   a. Locate familiar word parts, then locate the consonants.
   b. Locate the consonants, then locate the vowels.
   c. Locate the vowels, then locate familiar word parts.
   d. Look it up in the dictionary, then write down the meaning.

Read the following story, then answer the following questions that follow.

The kindergarten teacher is concerned about three of her students. While they are enthusiastic about writing, they do not always recognize letters, confusing b, d, and p, or e and o. They do, however, know which sounds go with certain letters when they are orally drilled. When they write, they appear to be attempting letter–sound associations.

"Now I'm writing *M*," the teacher heard one boy say as he scripted a large *N* in the upper right corner of his paper. He studied it for a moment and added, "Nope, it needs another leg." The student then wrote an *I* beside the *N*. "There," he said. "Now you are an *M*. I can write the word, 'man,' because now I have *M*." The child then moved to the lower left corner of the paper. "M-A-N," he said to himself, slowly pronouncing each sound. "I already have that *M*. Here is where the rest of the word goes." He turned the paper sideways and wrote *N*.

The second child sang to herself as she gripped the crayon and scribbled lines here and there on her paper. Some of the lines resembled letters, but few actually were. Others were scribbles. As she "wrote," she seemed to be making up a story and seemed to believe she was writing the story down.

The third child didn't vocalize at all while he worked. He gripped the paper and carefully wrote the same letter over and over and over. Sometimes the letter was large, sometimes tiny. He turned the paper in every direction so that sometimes the letter was sideways or upside down. Sometimes he flipped it backward. "What are you writing?" the teacher asked him. "My name," the child told her. The teacher then realized the letter was, indeed, the first letter of his name. She gently told him he had done a fine job of writing the first letter of his name. Did he want her to help him write the rest of it? "Nope," he cheerfully told her, "it's all here." He pointed at one of the letters and "read" his full name. He pointed at another letter and again seemed to believe it represented all the sounds of his name.

33. The kindergarten teacher isn't certain if these children are exhibiting signs of a reading disability or other special needs. What should the teacher do?
   a. Nothing. These children are simply at an early stage in the reading/writing process.
   b. Nothing. She doesn't want to have to tell the parents that their children are sub-par in terms of intelligence. They are perfectly nice children and can contribute to society in other ways. She resolves to give them extra attention in other areas to help them build confidence.
   c. She should recommend that the parents take the children to be tested for a number of reading disorders, including dyslexia.
   d. She should arrange a meeting between herself, the school psychologist, and the reading specialist to discuss the matter and resolve it using a three-pronged approach.

34. In the above example, the emergent writers are demonstrating their understanding that letters symbolize predictable sounds, that words begin with an initial sound/letter, and that by "writing," they are empowering themselves by offering a reader access to their thoughts and ideas. The next three stages the emergent writers will pass through in order will most likely be:
   a. Scripting the end-sound to a word (KT=cat); leaving space between words; writing from the top left to the top right of the page, and from top to bottom.
   b. Scripting the end-sound to a word (KT=cat); writing from the top left to the top right of the page, and from top to bottom; separating the words from one another with a space between.
   c. Leaving space between the initial letters that represent words; writing from the top left to the top right of the page, and from top to bottom; scripting the final sound of each word as well as the initial sound (KT=cat).
   d. Drawing a picture beside each of the initial sounds to represent the entire word; scripting the end-sound to a word (KT=cat); scripting the interior sounds that compose the entire word (KAT=cat).

35. The teacher might best encourage the three students in the above example by:
   a. Suggesting they write an entire book rather than just a single page. This will build confidence, teach them sequencing, and encourage the young writers to delve deeper into their ideas.
   b. Ask the students to read their stories to her. Suggest they visit other children in the class and read to each of them.
   c. Contact the local newspaper and invite a reporter to visit her class and write a story about her emergent writers. In this way, they are sure to see themselves as "real writers" and will more fully apply themselves to the task.
   d. Invite all the parents to visit the class the following week. This will give all classmates, regardless of where they are on the learning spectrum, time to memorize their stories. The children will be very excited and will begin to see themselves as "real writers."

36. At what point should the kindergarten teacher in the above example offer the three children picture books and ask them to read to her?
   a. When the three children are all able to script initial sounds, end sounds, and interior sounds they are ready to decode words. She should make her request at this point.
   b. As each child reaches the stage in which he or she can script initial sounds, end sounds, and interior sounds, the teacher should ask only that child to read to her.
   c. As each child reaches the stage in which he habitually writes from the top to the bottom of the page, moving left to right, the time has come. Books are intended to be read in this way, and until a child has had the experience of writing in the same manner, he won't be able to make sense of the words.
   d. The teacher should encourage all students to "read" picture books from the first day of school. Talking about the pictures from page to page gives young readers the idea that books are arranged sequentially. Pictures also offer narrative coherence and contextual clues. Emergent readers who are encouraged to enjoy books will more readily embrace the act of reading. Holding a book and turning pages gives young readers a familiarity with them.

37. How does a teacher most effectively teach spelling?
   a. Students who have a clear understanding of letter–sound association do not need to be taught to spell. If they can say a word, they can spell it.
   b. Students who have a clear understanding of letter–sound association, who can identify syllables, and who recognize when the base word is of Latin, Greek, or Indo-European ancestry do not need to be taught to spell. They can deduce what is most likely the correct spelling using a combination of these strategies. A teacher who posts charts organizing words into their ancestor families, phonemic units, and word-sound families is efficiently teaching spelling. The rest is up to the student.
   c. Students who spell poorly will be at a disadvantage for the rest of their lives. It is essential that students spend at least 15 minutes a day drilling spelling words until they know them forward and backward. The teacher should alternate between having students write a new word 25 times and having the entire class chant the spelling of the words.
   d. Students should be taught that writing is a process. By teaching students to apply spelling patterns found in common phonemic units, the spelling of many words can be deduced. Sight words that are high frequency and do not follow patterns found in other words (the, guardian, colonel) must be taught.

38. A teacher is teaching students analogizing. She is teaching them to:
   a. Identify and use metaphors.
   b. Identify and use similes.
   c. Identify and use groups of letters that occur in a word family.
   d. Identify and use figures of speech.

39. A reading teacher is working with a student who has just moved to Texas from Korea. The child knows very few words in English. The teacher offers her a picture book of Korean folk tales. Using words and gestures, the teacher asks her to "read" one folk tale. The child "reads" the familiar tale in Korean. The teacher then writes key English words on the board and asks the child to find those words in the book. When the child finds the words, they read them together. This strategy is:
   a. Useful. The child will feel more confident because the story is already familiar. She will also feel that the lesson is a conversation of sorts, and that she is communicating successfully. She will be motivated to learn the English words because they are meaningful and highly charged.
   b. Useful. The teacher is learning as much as the child is. The teacher is learning about Korean culture and language, and she can apply this knowledge when teaching future Korean students.
   c. Not very useful. The child needs to be exposed to as much American culture as possible. Encouraging her to remember her own culture will make her sad and will limit her curiosity about her new home.
   d. Not very useful. The first things the child should learn are the letters of the alphabet and associative sounds. Only then can she begin to decipher an unfamiliar language.

40. The teacher in the previous question was using what kind of load?
   a. Language load
   b. Cognitive load
   c. Bilingual load
   d. Cultural load

41. Using brain imaging, researchers have discovered that dyslexic readers use the _____ side(s) of their brains, while non-dyslexic readers use the _____ side(s) of their brains.
   a. Left; right
   b. Right; left
   c. Right and left; left
   d. Right; left and right

42. A fifth grader has prepared a report on reptiles, which is something he knows a great deal about. He rereads his report and decides to make a number of changes. He moves a sentence from the top to the last paragraph. He crosses out several words and replaces them with more specific words. He circles key information and draws an arrow to show another place the information could logically be placed. He is engaged in:
   a. Editing
   b. Revising
   c. First editing, then revising
   d. Reviewing

43. *Bi, re,* and *un* are:
   a. Suffixes, appearing at the beginning of base words to change their meaning.
   b. Suffixes, appearing at the end of base words to enhance their meaning.
   c. Prefixes, appearing at the beginning of base words to emphasize their meaning.
   d. Prefixes, appearing at the beginning of base words to change their meanings.

44. Examples of CVC words include:
    a. Add, pad, mad
    b. Cat, tack, act
    c. Elephant, piano, examine
    d. Dog, sit, leg

45. A teacher is working with a student who is struggling with reading. The teacher gives him a story with key words missing:

> The boy wanted to take the dog for a walk. The boy opened the door. The ____ ran out. The ___ looked for the dog. When he found the dog, he was very _____.

The student is able to fill in the blanks by considering:
    a. Syntax. Oftentimes, word order gives enough clues that a reader can predict what happens next.
    b. Pretext. By previewing the story, the student can deduce the missing words.
    c. Context. By considering the other words in the story, the student can determine the missing words.
    d. Sequencing. By putting the ideas in logical order, the student can determine the missing words.

46. The following is/are (an) element(s) of metacognition:
    a. A reader's awareness of herself as a learner.
    b. A reader's understanding of a variety of reading strategies and how to apply them to comprehend a text.
    c. A reader who is conscious about remembering what has been read.
    d. All of the above.

47. Collaborative Strategic Reading (CSR) is a teaching technique that depends on two teaching practices. These practices are:
    a. Cooperative learning and reading comprehension.
    b. Cooperative reading and metacognition.
    c. Reading comprehension and metacognition.
    d. Cooperative learning and metacognition.

48. Context cues are useful in:
    a. Predicting future action.
    b. Understanding the meaning of words that are not familiar.
    c. Understanding character motivation.
    d. Reflecting on a text's theme.

49. A teacher has a child who does not volunteer in class. When the teacher asks the student a question the student can answer, she does so with as few words as possible. The teacher isn't sure how to best help the child. She should:
   a. Leave the child alone. She is clearly very shy and will be embarrassed by having attention drawn to her. She is learning in her own way.
   b. Ask two or three highly social children to include this girl in their activities. She is shy, and she probably won't approach them on her own.
   c. Observe the child over the course of a week or two. Draw her into conversation and determine if her vocabulary is limited, if she displays emotional problems, or if her reticence could have another cause. Note how the child interacts with others in the class. Does she ever initiate conversation? If another child initiates, does she respond?
   d. Refer her to the school counselor immediately. It is clear the child is suffering from either a low IQ or serious problems at home.

50. A first grader is reading a book aloud. The teacher notes that the book uses word families. Some of the words are *fat, hat, sat, fit, hit, sit, run, fun, sun, hot, cot,* and *not.* The child ignores the pictures and attempts to read by identifying the rhyme. However, she frequently misreads, replacing the correct word with another from the same word family. The child needs:
   a. Encouragement. She will eventually understand.
   b. Intervention. She can identify groups of letters, but is not able to apply letter–sound association.
   c. To practice singing the alphabet.
   d. Nothing. This is a normal stage in the reading process.

51. A high school class reads an essay about the possible effects of sexual activity on teens. The author's position is very clear: She believes young people should avoid sex because they aren't mature enough to take the necessary steps to remain safe. The author cites facts, research studies, and statistics to strengthen her position. This type of writing is called:
   a. Expository
   b. Narrative
   c. Persuasive
   d. Didactic

52. A reading teacher feels that some of his strategies aren't effective. He has asked a specialist to observe him and make suggestions as to how he can improve. The reading specialist should suggest that first:
   a. The teacher set up a video camera and record several sessions with different students for the specialist to review. The presence of an observer changes the outcome; if the specialist is in the room, it will negatively affect the students' ability to read.
   b. The teacher reflect on his strategies himself. Which seem to work? Which don't? Can the teacher figure out why? It's always best to encourage teachers to find their own solutions so that they can handle future issues themselves.
   c. They meet to discuss areas the teacher is most concerned about and decide on the teacher's goals.
   d. The specialist should arrive unannounced to observe the teacher interacting with students. This will prevent the teacher from unconsciously overpreparing.

53. A kindergarten teacher pronounces a series of word pairs for her students. The students repeat the pairs. Some of the pairs rhyme (*see/bee*) and some of the pairs share initial sounds but do not rhyme (*sit, sun*). The students help her separate the word pairs into pairs that rhyme and pairs that do not. Once the students are able to distinguish between two words that rhyme and two words that do not, the teacher says a word and asks them to provide a rhyme. When she says *cat* a child responds with *fat*. When she says *sing* a child offers *thing*. How does this strictly oral activity contribute to the children's ability to read?
    a. It doesn't. Oral activities must have a written component to be useful to emergent readers.
    b. It is helpful in that it demonstrates how different sounds are made with different letters.
    c. It actually discourages children from reading. By emphasizing orality over literacy, the teacher is suggesting to the children that reading is not an important skill.
    d. Being able to identify rhyme is an important element of phonological awareness.

54. Syllable types include:
    a. Closed, open, silent e, vowel team, vowel-r, and consonant-le.
    b. Closed, open, silent, double-vowel, r, and le.
    c. Closed, midway, open, emphasized, prefixed, and suffixed.
    d. Stressed, unstressed, and silent.

55. An eighth-grade student is able to decode most words fluently and has a borderline/acceptable vocabulary, but his reading comprehension is quite low. He can be helped with instructional focus on:
    a. Strategies to increase comprehension and to build vocabulary.
    b. Strategies to increase comprehension and to be able to identify correct syntactical usage.
    c. Strategies to improve his understanding of both content and context.
    d. Strategies to build vocabulary and to improve his understanding of both content and context.

56. Reading comprehension and vocabulary can best be assessed:
    a. With brief interviews and tests every two months to determine how much learning has taken place. Students learn in spurts, and in-depth assessments of comprehension and vocabulary are a waste of time.
    b. Through a combination of standardized testing, informal teacher observations, attention to grades, objective-linked assessments, and systematized charting of data over time.
    c. By giving students weekly self-assessment rubrics to keep them constantly aware of and invested in their own progress.
    d. By having students retell a story or summarize the content of an informational piece of writing. The degree to which the material was comprehended, and the richness or paucity of vocabulary used in such work, provides efficient and thorough assessment.

57. An ORF is:
    a. An Oral Reading Fluency assessment.
    b. An Occasional Reading Function assessment.
    c. An Oscar Reynolds Feinstein assessment.
    d. An Overt Reading Failure assessment.

58. An outcome assessment is given:
   a. At the end of the year, to determine if instructional goals established at the beginning of the year have been successfully reached.
   b. At the beginning of the year to establish a point of reference for a series of regularly administered assessments throughout the year.
   c. When a student has finished a text to determine how clearly she understood the story's implied outcome.
   d. There is no such assessment.

59. Word-recognition ability is:
   a. Equally important to all readers.
   b. Used only by fluent readers.
   c. Another term for "word attack."
   d. Especially important to English Language Learners and students with reading disabilities.

60. Research indicates that developing oral language proficiency in emergent readers is important because:
   a. Proficiency with oral language enhances students' phonemic awareness and increases vocabulary.
   b. The more verbally expressive emergent readers are, the more confident they become. Such students will embrace both Academic and Independent reading levels.
   c. It encourages curiosity about others. With strong oral language skills, students begin to question the world around them. The more they ask, the richer their background knowledge.
   d. It demonstrates to students that their ideas are important and worth sharing.

61. In preparation for writing a paper, a high school class has been instructed to skim a number of Internet and print documents. They are being asked to:
   a. Read the documents several times, skimming to a deeper level of understanding each time.
   b. Read the documents quickly, looking for those that offer the most basic, general information.
   c. Read the documents quickly, looking for key words in order to gather the basic premise of each.
   d. Read the documents carefully, looking for those that offer the most in-depth information.

62. The students in the above question are most likely preparing to write a(n) _____ essay:
   a. Personal
   b. Expository
   c. Literary
   d. Narrative

A teacher has given the first paragraph of an essay to her students to analyze and discuss. Read the paragraph and answer the following questions:

Americans have struggled with cigarettes far too long. Until now, it has been a personal choice to smoke (or not), but the time for change is rapidly approaching. Local legislation has already begun for schools, restaurants, arenas, and other public places to be smoke-free. Years ago cigarette smoking was presented by the media as being fashionable, even sexy. In magazines, movies, and later in television, celebrities would indulge themselves with a smoke and even be paid to endorse a brand. As recently as 1975, it was common for talk show hosts like Tom Snyder and Johnny Carson to keep a cigarette burning. Cigarette smoking in America has persisted in spite of frightening concerns like lung cancer and emphysema. Over the years, the tobacco industry has sought to diffuse strong evidence that smoking is harmful. However, the myth of "safe cigarettes," questions about nicotine addiction, and denials about the dangers of secondhand smoke have proven to be propaganda and lies.

63. This is a(n) _____ essay:
    a. Compare/contrast
    b. Persuasive
    c. Narrative
    d. Analytic

64. The thesis statement is:
    a. However, the myth of "safe cigarettes," questions about nicotine addiction, and denials about the dangers of secondhand smoke have proven to be propaganda and lies.
    b. Americans have struggled with cigarettes far too long.
    c. Until now, it has been a personal choice to smoke (or not), but the time for change is rapidly approaching.
    d. In magazines, movies, and later in television, celebrities would indulge themselves with a smoke and even be paid to endorse a brand.

65. The next three paragraphs in the essay will most likely address:
    a. Smoking as a personal choice, changes in local legislation, and how fashionable smoking once was.
    b. How fashionable smoking once was, talk show hosts smoking on air, the myth of "safe cigarettes."
    c. Propaganda and lies, the myth of "safe cigarettes," and how long Americans have struggled with cigarettes.
    d. The myth of "safe cigarettes," questions about nicotine addiction, and the dangers of secondhand smoke.

66. The teacher and her students brainstorm a list of talents, skills, and specialized knowledge belonging to members of the class. Some of the items on the list include how to make a soufflé, how to juggle, and how to teach a dog to do tricks. One student knows a great deal about spiders, and another about motorcycles. She asks each student to write an essay about something he or she is good at or knows a great deal about. What kind of essay is she asking the students to produce?
    a. Cause and effect
    b. Compare/contrast
    c. Example
    d. Argumentative

67. *Caret, carrot, to, two and too* share something in common. They:
    a. Are nouns.
    b. Are monosyllabic.
    c. Are homophones.
    d. Represent things in nature.

Read the following paragraph, then answer the questions that follow:
    A class will visit an assisted living facility to interview residents about their lives. Each group of three has selected a theme such as love, work, or personal accomplishment and written several questions around that theme. Next, each group practices interviewing one another. The teacher then asks all the students to discuss the questions that caused them to respond most thoughtfully, as well as those they were less inspired by. The students decided the questions that were easiest to respond to asked for very specific information; for example, one inspiring question was, "Please tell me about something you learned to do as a child that affected the direction of your life." Those that were uninspiring were too broad, for example, "Please tell me about your happiest memory."

68. After they interview the residents, each group of three students will work together to write a piece about the resident. This kind of approach is called:
    a. Collaborative learning
    b. Companion learning
    c. Bonded learning
    d. Group learning

69. The genre the teacher expects is:
    a. Memoir
    b. Historical fiction
    c. Biography
    d. Autobiography

70. The teacher wants the students to apply what they've learned across content areas. Which of the following strategies would be most effective?
    a. Students will interview a family member, asking the same questions.
    b. Students will write a personal piece in which they address the same questions.
    c. Students will do online research about the cultural, economic, or political events that were occurring during the specific time about which they've written.
    d. Students pretend to be the interviewee and rewrite the piece from a first person point of view.

Read the following paragraph, then respond to the questions that follow.
> A seventh-grade teacher asks the reading teacher to suggest a lesson students will find simultaneously challenging and fun. The reading teacher suggests the class read fairy tales from both Hans Christian Anderson and the Brothers Grimm and have a rapid-paced, energetic discussion about the many similarities and differences between the two while the teacher lists them on the board.

71. The individual strategies the students will employ are:
    a. Collaborative learning and genre.
    b. Brainstorming and a compare/contrast strategy.
    c. Collaborative learning and brainstorming.
    d. Analyzing and genre.

72. The lesson is asking the students to consider two different:
    a. Learning styles
    b. Genres
    c. Writing styles
    d. Reading styles

73. The primary benefit of this exercise is that it promotes students':
    a. Vocabulary
    b. Comprehension
    c. Fluency
    d. Word identification

74. The students enjoyed the assignment so much that the teacher suggested they select one fairy tale and modernize it without changing the basic structure. Evil kings and queens could become corrupt politicians; pumpkins could turn into Hummers, and romantic princes might reveal themselves as rock stars. The teacher believes this assignment will most effectively demonstrate to the students:
    a. The importance of setting to meaning.
    b. The importance of characters to meaning.
    c. The importance of culture to meaning.
    d. The importance of creativity to meaning.

75. The first-grade teacher wants her class to understand that stories have a certain order. She reads them a story, then orally reviews with them how each event that happened in the story caused the next event to happen. To reinforce the lesson the teacher should:
   a. Give each child a piece of drawing paper that has been folded in half and then again, creating four boxes, along with a piece that has not been folded. The teacher should then ask the students to draw a cartoon about the story. Each of the first four boxes will show the events in order. The second page is to show how the story ends.
   b. Give each child a piece of drawing paper and ask the students to draw the most important scene.
   c. Give each child a piece of drawing paper and ask the students to draw the story's beginning on the front of the page and ending on the back.
   d. Give each child a piece of drawing paper that has been folded in half and then again, creating four boxes, along with a piece that has not been folded. The teacher should then ask the students to draw a cartoon about anything they want. She reminds them to put their story cartoons in proper order.

76. A ninth grade class is reading a 14-line poem in iambic pentameter. There are three stanzas of four lines each, and a two-line couplet at the end. Words at the end of each line rhyme with another word in the same stanza. The class is reading a:
   a. Sonnet
   b. Villanelle
   c. Sestina
   d. Limerick

77. A teacher is working with a group of English Language Learners. She asks them to take two pieces of paper. At the top of the first paper they are to write *SAME*. At the top of the other, *DIFFERENT*. Each child will consider what his native country and the United States have in common, and what distinct features each country possesses. The children are using which method in organizing their ideas?
   a. Hunt and peck
   b. Consider and persuade
   c. Evaluate and contrast
   d. Compare and contrast

78. Next, the teacher in the previous story drew two overlapping circles on the board. She labeled one circle *MALI*. The other circle was labeled *U.S.* She labeled the overlap joining the two circles *SAME*. On the far side of each circle, she wrote *DIFFERENT*. In the *U.S.* circle, she wrote *many cars, very good roads, people live in big cities, many families have pets,* and *houses made of wood.* In the side labeled *MALI* she wrote *fewer cars, many broken roads, most people live in villages, animals are not pets,* and *houses made of mud.* What will she write in the third, overlapping area?
   a. Telephones, personal computers, cars, and apartment buildings.
   b. Dogs, cats, fish, and birds.
   c. People celebrate marriages, births, and historical events.
   d. Movies, *television, books*, and *Internet.*

79. What type of prewriting activity has the teacher in the previous example drawn on the board?
    a. A verbal diagram
    b. Thought bubbles
    c. A web
    d. A Venn diagram

80. A third grader knows he needs to write from left to right, and from top to bottom on the page. He knows what sounds are associated with specific letters. He can recognize individual letters and can hear word families. He correctly identifies prefixes, suffixes, and homonyms, and his reading comprehension is very good. However, when he is asked to write, he becomes very upset. He has trouble holding a pencil, his letters are very primitively executed, and his written work is not legible. He most likely has:
    a. Dysgraphia
    b. Dyslexia
    c. Dyspraxia
    d. Nonverbal learning disorder

81. The phrase "Pretty as a picture" is *best* described as a:
    a. Metaphor
    b. Cliché
    c. Simile
    d. Figure of speech

82. A fourth-grade teacher had her students write haiku in order to promote the students' _____.
    a. Reading comprehension
    b. Vocabulary
    c. Word identification skills
    d. Confidence

83. A second-grade teacher wants to help her students enrich their vocabulary. She's noticed that their writing journals are filled with serviceable but unexciting verbs such as "said" and "went," and general rather than specific nouns. The most effective lesson would involve:
    a. Suggesting students use a thesaurus to substitute more unusual words for common ones.
    b. Suggesting students add an adjective to each noun.
    c. Brainstorming a list of verbs that mean ways of talking or ways of going, then adding them to the word wall along with some nouns that specify common topics.
    d. Suggesting students look up the meanings of boring words and consider another way to express them.

84. At the beginning of the school year, a parent is concerned about her first-grade child. The child has a very good speaking vocabulary, but this is not reflected in her writing. She reads a little above grade level, but the parent feels the child "fakes it" by looking at the pictures and guessing based on the context of the story. The parent is concerned that the child is not reading so much as remembering what a book is about and filling in areas of confusion with guesses. The parent points to the child's writing samples as further evidence. The day before, the child scripted:

My famble will go to the fare on Saturday we will ride the farus will. We will eat popzikls. I want to win a stuft aminul. (*My family will go to the fair on Saturday. We will ride the Ferris wheel. We will eat popsicles. I want to win a stuffed animal.*)

The teacher:
   a. Shares the parent's concern. They meet with the resource teacher to set up a program to address the problems.
   b. Advocates a wait-and-see policy. It is very early in the school year, and young children often demonstrate very rapid growth in previously problematic areas.
   c. Explains to the parent that the child is not experiencing problems. She is correctly using the sight words she has learned, applying her knowledge of word families to determine spelling of similar words, and correctly hearing phonemes and scripting the words that represent them. Her strong verbal vocabulary and her reading skills are further evidence she is doing well. Her writing will catch up as she learns further strategies and sight words.
   d. Explains to the parent that the child is not experiencing problems. She is eager to memorize sight words, and the teacher feels certain that the student's writing will radically improve as she memorizes the correct the spellings of all the words she wants to write.

85. Examples of onomatopoeia are:
   a. Sink, drink, mink, link.
   b. Their, there, they're.
   c. Drip, chirp, splash, giggle.
   d. *Think, in, thin, ink.*

86. "Code knowledge" facilitates reading fluency because:
   a. It brings the entirety of the student's previous experience to bear on decoding a text.
   b. It offers a framework for organizing new information by assigning code words to sets of ideas.
   c. There is no such thing as "code knowledge." The correct term is "core knowledge."
   d. It offers a systematic approach to untangling the wide variety of vowel sounds when an unfamiliar word is encountered.

87. The purpose of "targeted instruction" is to:
   a. Deliver instructions that are precise, clear, and direct so that students understand exactly what is expected.
   b. Accurately rank a group of learners from low achievers to high achievers so that the teacher knows from the beginning of the school year which students have less ability and will therefore need support.
   c. Teach students how to take information from a text and reorganize it into bulleted lists.
   d. Assess and target areas needing improvement as well as areas of greatest strength for each student to ensure that all members of a class are receiving instruction tailored to their specific needs.

88. Components of "explicit instruction" include:
   a. Clarifying the goal, modeling strategies, and offering explanations geared to a student's level of understanding.
   b. Determining the goal, offering strategies, and asking questions designed to ascertain whether understanding has been reached.
   c. Reassessing the goal, developing strategies, and determining whether further reassessing of the goal is required.
   d. Objectifying the goal, assessing strategies, and offering explanations geared toward a student's level of understanding.

89. A teacher has challenged a student with a book about Antarctica that is just beyond the high end of the student's Instructional level. The teacher points out that the student already knows quite a bit about penguins because the class studied them earlier in the year. He reminds the student that she's recently seen a television show about the seals that also live in Antarctic waters. The teacher gives the student a list of words she's likely to find in the text, and they discuss what those words might mean. The student begins to read, but stops to ask the teacher what *circumpolar* means. The teacher is also unfamiliar with the word, but reminds her that *circum* is a prefix. The student recalls that it means "about or around" and deduces that circumpolar most likely refers to something found around or in a polar region. This instructional approach is called:
   a. Modular instruction
   b. Scaffolding
   c. Linking
   d. Transmutation

90. The second graders are confused. They've learned to hear and count syllables. They understand that contractions such as *won't*, *didn't*, and *we're* represent two words converted into one. Now the teacher is trying to explain compound words. She has shown the children that a compound word is made of two words and has a meaning that is a little different from either of words that compose it. She pronounces *doghouse*, and asks if it is one word or two. "Two," the students correctly respond. The teacher now says *parent*. Again, the students tell her it's two words. The teacher explains there are two syllables but not two words. One child nods and says, "Like the word 'didn't.' That's two words but it sounds like one." What is the best way for the teacher to correct the students' misunderstanding?
   a. Point out compound words the children use throughout the day. Write them on the board, and ask students to list them in their writing journals.
   b. Assess the degree of confusion. Give the students a quiz listing a number of two-syllable words, compound words, and contractions. Ask the students to cross out the two-syllable words and contractions.
   c. Write a compound word such as doghouse on the board. Underline dog, and then house. Beneath the words draw a picture of a dog and a house, joined with a plus sign. Next, write another compound word and ask the class to draw the pictures in their journals. Give the students a handout with several compound words. Ask them to underline the two words, then to draw the pictures.
   d. Turn the lesson into fun by suggesting the students invent new compound words. Demonstrate by inventing one such as nosemitten instead of scarf. Children learn more readily when they are enjoying it.

91. An understanding of the meanings of prefixes and suffixes such as *dis, mis, un, re, able,* and *ment* are important for:
   a. Reading comprehension
   b. Word recognition
   c. Vocabulary building
   d. Reading fluency

92. VC, CVC, CCVC, CVCC, and CCVCC are among the types of:
   a. Homophones
   b. Closed syllables
   c. Monosyllabic words
   d. Polyglotal indicators

93. A student is taking a reading test. The teacher has blocked out a number of words. Each blank is assigned a set of three possible words. The student must select the correct word from each set so that the text makes sense. The student is taking:
   a. A cloze test
   b. A maze test
   c. A multiple-choice quiz
   d. A vocabulary test

94. When working with English Language Learners, the teacher should:
   a. Avoid idioms and slang, involve students in hands-on activities, reference students' prior knowledge, and speak slowly.
   b. Speak slowly, use monosyllabic words whenever possible, repeat each sentence three times before moving to the next sentence, and employ idioms but not slang.
   c. Use monosyllabic words whenever possible, repeat key instructions three times but not in a row, reference students' prior knowledge, and have students keep a journal of new vocabulary.
   d. Have students keep a journal of new vocabulary, reference students' prior knowledge, speak slowly, and involve students in hands-on activities.

95. Editing involves:
   a. Correcting surface features such as sentence fragments, spelling, and punctuation.
   b. Fine-tuning the underlying structure of the piece to make the theme stand out.
   c. Reconsidering ideas, adding or subtracting information, and changing the underlying structure.
   d. Adding illustrations, charts, and other useful addenda.

96. A seventh grader has never had much success with reading. Her ability to decode is rudimentary; she stops and starts when reading, frequently loses her place, or misreads an important word. She doesn't seem aware of where errors occur, or she does not attempt to correct them. When asked to tell about what she's read, her comprehension is minimal. To help her, instructional focus on which of the following would be most useful?
   a. Carefully organized lessons in decoding, sight words, vocabulary, and comprehension at least three to five times a week. These mini-lessons must be extremely clear, with the parts broken down to the lowest common denominator. The more tightly interwoven and systematized the instruction, the better chance this student will have.
   b. A weekly lesson focusing on one aspect of reading. This student will be overwhelmed if too many strategies are offered at once. The instruction should focus first on recognizing sight words, then letter–sound association. Next, the girl needs an understanding of the rules of syntax.
   c. The student isn't trying. Her instruction should be aimed at helping her learn to be self-motivated and disciplined in her approach to learning.
   d. Comprehension strategies will help her grasp the overall meaning of a text. From there she can begin to drill down until she's able to combine various approaches that, working together, will enable her to read.

97. Silent reading fluency can best be assessed by:
   a. Having the student retell or summarize the material to determine how much was understood.
   b. Giving a written test that covers plot, theme, character development, sequence of events, rising action, climax, falling action, and outcome. A student must test at a 95% accuracy rate to be considered fluent at silent reading.
   c. Giving a three-minute Test of Silent Contextual Reading Fluency four times a year. The student is presented with text in which spaces between words and all punctuation have been removed. The student must divide one word from another with slash marks, as in the following example: The/little/sailboat/bobbed/so/far/in/the/distance/it/looked/like/a/toy. The more words a student accurately separates, the higher her silent reading fluency score.
   d. Silent reading fluency cannot be assessed. It is a private act between the reader and the text and does not invite critique.

98. A high school teacher has given her students an assignment to write a non-rhyming poem of three lines. The first and last lines each contain five syllables, and the middle line contains seven syllables. The students are writing a:
   a. Limerick
   b. Metaphor
   c. Villanelle
   d. Haiku

99. "Verbal dyspraxia" refers to:
   a. Trouble with the physical act of writing.
   b. Confusing word or sentence order while speaking.
   c. Misplacement of letters within words.
   d. An inability to process verbal information.

100. "Coarticulation" affects:
   a. Blending awareness
   b. Phonemic awareness
   c. Sequencing
   d. Aural awareness

Answer Explanations

1. The answer is a: Homophones. Homophones are a type of homonym that sound alike, but are spelled differently and have different meanings. Other examples are *two, to,* and *too; their, they're,* and *there.*

2. The answer is c: Argumentative essay. The goal of a persuasive essay is to convince the reader that the author's position or opinion on a controversial topic is correct. That opinion or position is called the argument. A persuasive essay argues a series of points, supported by facts and evidence.

3. The answer is d: Rate, accuracy, and prosody. Fluent readers are able to read smoothly and comfortably at a steady pace (rate). The more quickly a child reads, the greater the chance of leaving out a word or substituting one word for another (for example, *sink* instead of *shrink*). Fluent readers are able to maintain accuracy without sacrificing rate. Fluent readers also stress important words in a text, group words into rhythmic phrases, and read with intonation (prosody).

4. The answer is b: The number of unrecognizable words an English Language Learner encounters when reading a passage or listening to a teacher. Language load is one of the barriers English Language Learners face. To lighten this load, a teacher can rephrase, eliminate unnecessary words, divide complex sentences into smaller units, and teach essential vocabulary before the student begins the lesson.

5. The answer is a: A vowel. A syllable is a minimal sound unit arranged around a vowel. For example, *academic* has four syllables: *a/ca/dem/ic.* It is possible for a syllable to be a single vowel, as in the above example. It is not possible for a syllable to be a single consonant.

6. The answer is c: Fail, producing students at a Frustration reading level. Those reading below grade level are likely to give up entirely. Those reading at grade level are likely to get frustrated and form habits that will actually slow down their development. Giving students texts that are too far beyond their reach produces frustrated readers. In an effort to succeed, frustrated writers are likely to apply strategies that have worked for them in the past but cannot work in this case because the text is simply beyond them. Looking for contextual clues to understand the meaning of unfamiliar words requires that most of the words in the passage are familiar. Breaking unfamiliar words into individual phonemes or syllables can be effective, but not if the number of such words is excessive. In this case, students below reading level and students at reading level will become frustrated when the skills that have worked for them in the past now fail.

7. The answer is c: Tier-two words. Tier-two words are words that are used with high frequency across a variety of disciplines or words with multiple meanings. They are characteristic of mature language users. Knowing these words is crucial to attaining an acceptable level of reading comprehension and communication skills.

8. The answer is c: Reading at her Independent reading level. When reading independently, students are at the correct level if they read with at least 97% accuracy.

9. The answer is b: To correct an error in reading a student has made, specifically clarifying where and how the error was made so that the student can avoid similar errors in the future. A reading teacher offers corrective feedback to a student in order to explain why a particular error in reading is, in fact, an error. Corrective feedback is specific; it locates where and how the student went astray so that similar errors can be avoided in future reading.

10. The answer is c: Content-specific words. Because these words are specific to paleontology, it's unlikely the students know their meanings. Without understanding what these words mean, the students would not be able to understand the content of the passage they were about to read.

11. The answer is b: Prior knowledge is knowledge the student brings from previous life or learning experiences to the act of reading. It is not possible for a student to fully comprehend new knowledge without first integrating it with prior knowledge. Prior knowledge, which rises from experience and previous learning, provides a framework by which new knowledge gained from the act of reading can be integrated. Every act of reading enriches a student's well of prior knowledge and increases that student's future ability to comprehend more fully any new knowledge acquired through reading.

12. The answer is b: Understanding of context and vocabulary. In a cloze test, a reader is given a text with certain words blocked out. The reader must be able to determine probable missing words based on contextual clues. In order to supply these words, the reader must already know them.

13. The answer is a: Common words with irregular spelling. Sight words occur in many types of writing; they are high-frequency words. Sight words are also words with irregular spelling. Some examples of sight words include *talk, some,* and *the.* Fluent readers need to recognize these words visually.

14. The answer is d: Consonant digraph. A consonant digraph is group of consonants in which all letters represent a single sound.

15. The answer is a: Phonological awareness. Phonemic awareness is the ability to recognize sounds within words. Segmenting words and blending sounds are components of phonemic awareness. Phonological awareness includes an understanding of multiple components of spoken language. Ability to hear individual words within a vocalized stream and ability to identify spoken syllables are types of phonological awareness.

16. The answer is a: Letter–sound correspondence. Letter–sound correspondence relies on the relationship between a spoken sound or group of sounds and the letters conventionally used in English to write them.

17. The answer is a: Strategy instruction. Strategic instruction involves teaching a methodic approach to solving a reading problem. It consists of strategies done in steps which aid the reader in eliminating incorrect responses.

18. The answer is d: Familiar, frequently used words that do not need to be taught beyond primary grades. Common or basic words are the first tier of three-tier words. These words are widely used across the spoken and written spectrum. Some examples are *walk, go, wish, the, look, happy,* and *always.* This essential vocabulary is taught early in a reader's instruction, and beyond that it need not be taught.

19. The answer is b: The number of phonemes. A phoneme is the smallest measure of language sound. English language phonemes, about 40 in number, are composed of individual letters as well as letter combinations. A number of letters have more than one associated sound. For example, "c" can be pronounced as a hard "c" (cake) or a soft "c" (Cynthia). Vowels in particular have a number of possible pronunciations.

20. The answer is b: Consonant blend. Consonant blend refers to a group of consonants in which each letter represents a separate sound.

21. The answer is a: Fewer than 100 words in the time given. At the beginning of the school year, second-grade students should be able to read 50–80 words per minute. By the time they are well into the school year, second-grade-level reading is tracked at 85 words per minute.

22. The answer is d: None; sight words cannot be decoded. Readers must learn to recognize these words as wholes on sight. Sight words have irregular spelling. Segmenting them into syllables or using a phonemic approach are ineffective strategies to aid a reader in recognizing a sight word, because these approaches depend on rules a sight word doesn't follow. Word families group words that share common patterns of consonants and vowels. The spelling of those words is therefore regular, because they follow a predictable pattern. Sight words are irregular and do not follow a predictable pattern and must be instantaneously recognized for writing fluency. No decoding is useful.

23. The answer is d: A and B. English Language Learners are simultaneously learning to read in English and to apply patterns of intonation that are likely different from those of their first languages. While it's often useful to arrange reading time with a family member, in this particular case reading with a family member who is not a fluent English speaker may reinforce intonation patterns and pronunciation that are not correct. Therefore, C is not the answer. Both A and B afford English Language Learners the opportunity to become familiar with reading rates that are appropriate to the text and simultaneously expose them to prosody. They will not only see text, but will hear proper intonation patterns that are likely different than those of their first languages.

24. The answer is c: Alphabetic principle. The act of decoding involves first recognizing the sounds individual letters and letter groups make, and then blending the sounds to read the word. A child decoding the word *spin,* for example, would first pronounce *sp/i/n* as individual sound units. She then would repeat the sounds, smoothly blending them. Because decoding involves understanding letters and their sounds, it is sometimes known as the alphabetic principle.

25. The answer is c: Events. "Reading" a story's illustrations offers visual clues to characters and events in the proper order. A story's plot is what happens first, next, later, and finally.

26. The answer is a: Oral. Phonological awareness refers to an understanding of the sounds a word makes. While phonological awareness leads to fluent reading skills, activities designed to develop an awareness of word sounds are, by definition, oral.

27. The answer is b: Vocabulary. Strategizing in order to understand the meaning of a word, knowing multiple meanings of a single word, and applying background knowledge to glean a word's meaning are all ways in which an effective reader enhances vocabulary. Other skills include an awareness of word parts and word origins, the ability to apply word meanings in a variety of content areas, and a delight in learning the meanings of unfamiliar words.

28. The answer is c: She is reading at an Instructional level. In one minute, a student who misreads one or less than one word per twenty words, or with 95%–100% accuracy, is at an Independent reading level. A student who misreads one or less than one word per ten words, or with 90%–95% accuracy, is at an Instructional level. A student misreading more than one word out of ten, or with less than 90% accuracy, is at a Frustration level.

29. The answer is d: Decoding depends on an understanding of letter–sound relationships. As soon as a child understands enough letters and their correspondent sounds to read a few words, decoding should be introduced. The act of decoding involves first recognizing the sounds individual letters and letter groups in a word make and then blending the sounds to read the word. It's important to introduce the strategy as soon as a child knows enough letters and their corresponding sounds to read simple words.

30. The answer is c: Cause–effect words. Signal words give the reader hints about the purpose of a particular passage. Some signal words are concerned with comparing/contrasting, some with cause and effect, some with temporal sequencing, some with physical location, and some with a problem and its solution. The words *since, whether,* and *accordingly* are words used when describing an outcome. Outcomes have causes.

31. The answer is a: Outcome. Story action can be analyzed in terms of rising action, story climax, falling action, and resolution. Rising action consists of those events that occur before and lead up to the story's most dramatic moment, or climax. The climax occurs toward the end of the book, but rarely, if ever, right at the end. Following the climax, the consequences of that dramatic moment are termed falling action. The story reaches resolution with the outcome of the falling action.

32. The answer is c: Locate the vowels, then locate familiar word parts. Syllables are organized around vowels. In order to determine the syllables, this student should begin by locating the vowels. It's possible to have a syllable that is a single vowel (*a/gain)*. It isn't possible to have a syllable that is a single consonant. Once the word has been broken into its component syllables the reader is able to study the syllables to find ones that are familiar and might give her a clue as to the word's meaning, such as certain prefixes or suffixes.

33. The answer is a: Nothing. These children are simply at an early stage in the reading/writing process. When emergent readers become aware of the connections between letters and sounds, and between reading and writing, they want to practice the skills they see proficient readers use. While a proficient writer knows that letters are grouped into words and that words are constructed into sentences that move from left to right and from the top of the page to the bottom, an emergent reader/writer knows only

that letters magically contain sounds that other people can read. It is necessary for children to pass through early stages in which they scribble-write and pretend they are scripting letters, which leads to a stage in which they actually do write the initial letter of a word all over the page. Next, the emergent reader/writer will write the initial letter of many of the words that belong in the sentence and will write them sequentially. KJM, for example, might mean *the cat chased a mouse.*

34. The answer is a: Scripting the end-sound to a word (KT=cat); leaving space between words; writing from the top left to the top right of the page, and from top to bottom. Each of these steps is progressively more abstract. Scripting the end-sound to a word helps a young writer recognize that words have beginnings and endings. This naturally leads to the willingness to separate words with white space so that they stand as individual entities. Once this step is reached, the child realizes that in English, writing progresses from left to right and from the top of the page to the bottom.

35. The answer is b: Ask the students to read their stories to her. Suggest they visit other children in the class and read to each of them. The teacher should encourage these students by "reading" what they have written, even if what she reads is incorrect. She might misread KJM as *Kathy jumped rope with Mandy.* Most children will not be upset by this, but will correct the teacher's misreading by reading what the letters really mean.

36. The answer is d: The teacher should encourage all students to "read" picture books from the first day of school. Talking about the pictures from page to page gives young readers the idea that books are arranged sequentially. Pictures also offer narrative coherence and contextual clues. Emergent readers who are encouraged to enjoy books will more readily embrace the act of reading. Holding a book and turning pages gives young readers a familiarity with them.

37. The answer is d: Students should be taught that writing is a process. By teaching students to apply spelling patterns found in common phonemic units, the spelling of many words can be deduced. Sight words that are high frequency and do not follow patterns found in other words (*the, guardian, colonel)* must be taught.

38. The answer is c: Identify and use groups of letters that occur in a word family. Analogizing is based on recognizing the pattern of letters in words that share sound similarities. If the pattern is found at the end of a family of words, it is called a *rhyme.* Some examples of rhyme are *rent, sent, bent,* and *dent.* If the pattern is found at the beginning of the family of words, it is frequently a consonant *blend* such as *street, stripe,* or *strong,* in which all the letters are pronounced, or the pattern is a consonant digraph, in which the letters are taken together to represent a single sound such as in *phone, phonics,* or *phantom.*

39. The answer is a: Useful. The child will feel more confident because the story is already familiar. She will also feel that the lesson is a conversation of sorts, and that she is communicating successfully. She will be motivated to learn the English words because they are meaningful and highly charged. As a newly arrived immigrant, the child feels overwhelmed. Presenting her with a book of folk tales from her country tells her that she needn't lose her culture in order to function in this one. It also comforts her by reminding her that her past and present are linked. Allowing her to speak in Korean helps her express herself without fear of judgment or failure. Presenting her with an English vocabulary that

is meaningful ensures that she will eagerly embrace these words, her first words in her new language.

40. The answer is d: Cultural load. Cultural load is concerned with how the relationship between language and culture can help or hinder learning. By using the Korean folk tale, the teacher offered the child the opportunity to learn new words in a context that was culturally familiar. By demonstrating respect for her student's culture, she helped lighten the cultural load.

41. The answer is c: Right and left; left. Researchers have discovered through brain imaging that a dyslexic reader uses both sides of the brain. Non-dyslexic readers use only the left side.

42. The answer is b: Revising. Revision (literally, re+vision) is the act of "seeing again." When revising, writers examine what they have written in order to improve the meaning of the work. Fine-tuning word choices, moving information to another location, and adding or deleting words are all acts of revision.

43. The answer is d: Prefixes, appearing at the beginning of base words to change their meanings. Suffixes appear at the end of words. Prefixes are attached to the beginning of words to change their meanings. *Un+happy, bi+monthly,* and *re+examine* are prefixes that, by definition, change the meanings of the words to which they are attached.

44. The answer is d: Dog, sit, leg. CVC words are composed of a consonant, a vowel, and a consonant. To learn to read them, students must be familiar with the letters used and their sounds. A teacher can present a word like *sit* to students who also know the consonants *b/f/h/p* and ask them to create a word family of other CVC words. The students will be able to read *bit, fit, hit,* and *pit* because they are similar to the word *sit* they have just learned.

45. The answer is c: Context. By considering the other words in the story, the student can determine the missing words. The student is depending on the information supplied by the rest of the story. This information puts the story into context.

46. The answer is d: All of the above. Metacognition means a reader's awareness of her own reading processes as she improves reading comprehension. Other elements of metacognition include awareness of areas in the text where the reader fails to comprehend and an understanding of how the text is structured.

47. The answer is a: Cooperative learning and reading comprehension. Cooperative learning occurs when a group of students at various levels of reading ability have goals in common. Reading comprehension is achieved through reading both orally and silently, developing vocabulary, a reader's ability to predict what will occur in a piece of writing, a reader's ability to summarize the main points in a piece of writing, and a reader's ability to reflect on the text's meaning and connect that meaning to another text or personal experience.

48. The answer is b: Understanding the meaning of words that are not familiar. Context cues offer insight into the probable meaning of unfamiliar words.

49. The answer is c: Observe the child over the course of a week or two. Draw her into conversation and determine if her vocabulary is limited, if she displays emotional problems, or if her reticence could have another cause. Note how the child interacts with others in the class. Does she ever initiate conversation? If another child initiates, does she respond? Until the teacher monitors the child's verbal abilities and habits, she cannot determine if the lack of interaction suggests a learning disability, an emotional problem, or simply a shy personality. The teacher should informally observe the child over a period of time, noting if and when she initiates or responds to oral language, if she is reading with apparent comprehension, if her vocabulary is limited, and the degree to which the child is interested in understanding.

50. The answer is b: Intervention. She can identify groups of letters, but is not able to apply letter–sound association. By first grade, a child should understand how to use word families to decode words. It is good that she can recognize the rhymes (common letter groups at the end of a word), but the fact that she does not know sounds associated with the letters that begin the word is troubling. She needs focused help on strengthening her ability to identify words.

51. The answer is c: Persuasive. The author is hoping to persuade or convince readers to avoid alcohol and tobacco by providing them with facts as well as by using rhetorical devices such as dispelling opposing arguments.

52. The answer is c: They meet to discuss areas the teacher is most concerned about and decide on the teacher's goals. In order to best achieve goals, those goals must be understood and established.

53. The answer is d: Being able to identify rhyme is an important element of phonological awareness. Young children use language in a solely oral way. Oral language is composed of separate sounds that are represented in written form by the alphabet. In order to read, a child must first have a sense of the sounds that are used in English (phonological awareness). By helping children hear the difference between rhyming and non-rhyming words, the teacher is preparing them to make the transition to sound–letter association and word families.

54. The answer is a: Closed, open, silent *e*, vowel team, vowel-*r*, and consonant-*le*. A closed syllable ends with a consonant, such as *cat*. Open syllables end with a vowel, such as *he*. Vowel team syllables contain two vowels working together, such as *main*. Vowel-*r* syllables such as *er* and *or* frequently occur as suffixes. Consonant-*le* syllables also typically occur as suffixes, such as *battle* or *terrible*.

55. The answer is a: Strategies to increase comprehension and to build vocabulary. The student should receive instruction focused on just those areas in which he is exhibiting difficulty. Improved vocabulary will give him greater skill at comprehending the meaning of a particular text. Strategies focused on enhancing comprehension together with a stronger vocabulary will provide the greatest help.

56. The answer is b: Through a combination of standardized testing, informal teacher observations, attention to grades, objective-linked assessments, and systematized charting of data over time. Reading comprehension and vocabulary cannot be sufficiently assessed with occasional, brief studies. Continuous observation, high-stakes and standardized

testing, attention to grades, and closely tracking the outcomes of objective-linked assessments are interrelated tools that, when systematically organized, offer a thorough understanding of students' strengths and weaknesses.

57. The answer is a: An Oral Reading Fluency assessment. ORF stands for oral reading fluency. This assessment measures the words correct per minute (WCPM) by subtracting the number of errors made from the total number of words orally read in a one- to two-minute period of time. It is used to find a student's Instructional reading level, to identify readers who are having difficulties, and to track developing fluency and word recognition over time.

58. The answer is a: At the end of the year, to determine if instructional goals established at the beginning of the year have been successfully reached. An outcome assessment given at the end of the year helps the reading teacher determine which students have reached instructional goals and do not need further support and which students will benefit from continued support.

59. The answer is d: Especially important to English Language Learners and students with reading disabilities. Word recognition is required for reading fluency and is important to all readers, but it is especially so to English Language Learners and students with reading disabilities. It can be effectively taught through precisely calibrated word study instruction designed to provide readers with reading and writing strategies for successful word analysis.

60. The answer is a: Proficiency with oral language enhances students' phonemic awareness and increases vocabulary. Understanding that words are scripted with specific letters representing specific sounds is essential to decoding a text. Students cannot effectively learn to read without the ability to decode. An enhanced vocabulary supports the act of reading; the larger an emergent reader's vocabulary, the more quickly he will learn to read. He will be able to decode more words, which he can organize into word families, which he can use to decode unfamiliar words.

61. The answer is c. Read the documents quickly, looking for key words in order to gather the basic premise of each. Skimming allows a reader to quickly gain a broad understanding of a piece of writing in order to determine if a more thorough reading is warranted. Skimming allows students who are researching a topic on the Internet or in print to consider a substantial body of information in order to select only that of particular relevance.

62. The answer is b. Expository. Expository essays clarify an idea, explain an event, or interpret facts. The position the author takes is often supported with statistics, quotations, or other evidence researched from a variety of sources.

63. The answer is b: Persuasive. A persuasive essay takes a strong position about a controversial topic and offers factual evidence to support this position. The goal of a persuasive paper is to convince the audience that the claim is true based on the evidence provided.

64. The answer is a: However, the myth of "safe cigarettes," questions about nicotine addiction, and denials about the dangers of secondhand smoke have proven to be

propaganda and lies. A thesis statement offers a hypothesis or opinion that the remainder of the paper then sets out to prove. Oftentimes, the thesis statement also offers a clear road map of the paper, foreshadowing the focuses of the paragraphs that follow and the order in which they will appear.

65. The answer is d. The myth of "safe cigarettes," questions about nicotine addiction, and the dangers of secondhand smoke. These three foci are presented in the thesis statement in this order and will be fleshed out in the following three paragraphs as the body of the essay.

66. The answer is c. Example. Example essays, also called illustration essays, are simple, straightforward pieces that depend on clearly described examples to make their points. An example essay isn't trying to convince the reader (argumentative), compare similar or dissimilar things (compare/contrast), or point to relationships such as cause and effect. Often, example essays teach the reader how to accomplish something or about something.

67. The answer is c: Are homophones. Homophones are words that are pronounced the same, but differ in meaning. For example, a bride wears a 2 caret ring, but a horse eats a carrot.

68. The answer is a: Collaborative learning. A group of students working together on a project are applying numerous learning strategies at once. Collaborative learning is a hands-on approach that actively involves students in the learning process. Students involved in collaborative learning typically retain the lesson better.

69. The answer is c: Biography. A biography relates information about part of the life of an individual. An autobiography is a biography about the writer's own life. A memoir is also autobiographical, but focuses on a theme. Historical fiction uses a setting or event based in historical fact as the background for characters and/or action that is invented.

70. The answer is c: Students will do online research about the cultural, economic, or political events that were occurring during the specific time about which they've written. By researching the historic setting that cradled the events their interviewee discussed, students are simultaneously broadening their understanding of the context and working in a different content area.

71. The answer is b. Brainstorming and a compare/contrast strategy. Brainstorming is a prewriting activity in which an individual or group responds to a specific question by considering any and all responses that arise without editing, prioritizing, or selecting. Once the brainstorming session is complete, students look at the results and eliminate any responses that are not useful, then group and prioritize the remaining responses. In this example, the students are having a collaborative learning experience in that they are brainstorming together; however, collaborative learning is not a strategy per se, but is the outcome of a strategy. The students are also employing a compare/contrast strategy in that they are looking both at how the two writing styles share common elements and how they are distinct.

72. The answer is c. Writing styles. Both Anderson and the Grimms wrote in the same genre, that of fairy tales. Genre refers to types of writing. Mystery, romance, adventure, historical fiction, and fairy tales are some examples of genres. A genre can include many different

authors and writing styles. These students are being asked to compare two distinct writing styles within a single genre in order to locate similarities and differences.

73. The answer is b. Comprehension. This exercise requires students to examine the authors' use of setting, plot, pacing, word choice, syntactical structures, narration, mood, metaphors, point of view, voice, and character development to find ways in which they are similar as well as different. In so doing, the students are discovering that language shapes meaning in ways both subtle and profound.

74. The answer is c: The importance of culture to meaning. Authors make thousands of decisions in the act of writing. What point of view to take, how much weight to give an event, what to reveal about a character, and what words will most effectively express the writer's intention are but a few of these decisions. While many of these decisions are consciously artistic choices, many are unconscious and imbedded in the cultural expectations of time and place in which the author has lived. To understand a text to the fullest degree possible, it is necessary to read it with an eye to the cultural framework from whence it came.

75. The answer is a: Give each child a piece of drawing paper that has been folded in half and then again, creating four boxes, along with a piece that has not been folded. The teacher should then ask the students to draw a cartoon about the story. Each of the first four boxes will show the events in order. The second page is to show how the story ends. When a child is able to visually see the way a familiar story has unfolded, that child can find causal or thematic connections in the action that increases her comprehension of the story overall. Asking the class to draw a single picture or to draw the beginning and end doesn't sufficiently demonstrate the importance of order to meaning. While some first graders may be able to create their own cartoon stories that demonstrate a logical series of events, many first graders are not yet ready to organize thought into a linear progression.

76. The answer is a: Sonnet. There are three primary types of sonnets. The Shakespearean sonnet is specifically what these students are reading. A Spenserian sonnet is also composed of three four-line stanzas followed by a two-line couplet; however, the rhymes are not contained within each stanza but spill from one stanza to the next (*abab bcbc cdcd ee*). A Petrarchan sonnet divides into an eight-line stanza and a six-line stanza.

77. The answer is d: Compare and contrast. Asking children to write a list provides them with a visual model that is a side-by-side comparison of the two countries. In creating that visual model, each student first has to organize his or her thoughts mentally, deciding whether each particular item under consideration shares more or less in common with the other.

78. The answer is c: *People celebrate marriages, births, and historical events.* The overlapping area is reserved for those items that are not culturally specific but are seen in both cultures.

79. The answer is d. A Venn diagram. A Venn diagram uses two or more circles with a common, overlapping area as a model to organize similar and dissimilar elements. The greater the number of similarities, the closer the circles must be and consequently, the greater the overlapping area. The fewer the number of similarities, the farther apart the circles will be and, consequently, the smaller the overlapping area.

80. The answer is a. Dysgraphia. Dysgraphic individuals have difficulty with the physical act of writing. They find holding and manipulating a pencil problematic. Their letters are primitively formed, and their handwriting is illegible.

81. The answer is b. Cliché. While "Pretty as a picture" is a simile (comparison of two unlike things using *like* or *as*), its overuse has turned it into a cliché. A cliché is a trite platitude.

82. The answer is b. Vocabulary. The tightly controlled syllabic requirements will cause students to search for words outside their normal vocabularies that will fit the rigid framework and still express the writer's intended meanings. Often, students will rediscover a word whose meaning they know, but they don't often use.

83. The answer is c. Brainstorming a list of verbs that mean ways of talking or ways of going, then adding them to the word wall along with some nouns that specify common topics. Second graders aren't developmentally ready for a thesaurus; most will believe that any words in a particular list are interchangeable. For example, a student who wrote *My little sister walks like a baby* might find the verbs *strut, sidle,* and *amble* in the thesaurus. None of these verbs would be an appropriate substitution. Supplementing a noun with an adjective often results in flat writing: *There's a tree in my yard* might become *There's a nice tree in my big yard.* Adjectives such as *pretty, fun, cute, funny,* and so forth don't add much in terms of meaning, but they are the adjectives younger writers reach for first. A more specific noun is both more meaningful and more interesting. *There's a weeping willow in my yard* is evocative.

84. The correct answer is c: Explains to the parent that the child is not experiencing problems. She is correctly using the sight words she has learned, applying her knowledge of word families to determine spelling of similar words, and correctly hearing phonemes and scripting the words that represent them. Her strong verbal vocabulary and her reading skills are further evidence she is doing well. Her writing will catch up as she learns further strategies and sight words.

85. The answer is c: *Drip, chirp, splash, giggle.* Onomatopoeia refers to words that sound like what they represent.

86. The answer is d: It offers a systematic approach to untangling the wide variety of vowel sounds when an unfamiliar word is encountered. Code knowledge, also called orthographic tendencies, is a helpful approach to decoding a word when multiple pronunciation possibilities exist. For example, in the words *toe, go, though,* and *low,* the long O sound is written in a variety of ways. A code knowledge approach teaches a reader to first try a short vowel sound. If that doesn't help, the reader should consider the different ways the vowel or vowel groups can be pronounced, based on what he knows about other words.

87. The answer is d: Assess and target areas needing improvement as well as areas of greatest strength for each student to ensure the all members of a class are receiving instruction tailored to their specific needs.

88. The answer is a: Clarifying the goal, modeling strategies, and offering explanations geared to a student's level of understanding. Explicit instruction is well organized and structured, and it offers easily understood steps and depends in part on frequent reference to previously learned materials.

89. The answer is b: Scaffolding. Using this strategic approach, a teacher assigns a task that is just beyond the student's current level. The teacher encourages the student's attempts at comprehension by offering various supports that largely depend on prior knowledge, in order to develop the student's willingness to move forward into uncharted territory as a confident independent learner.

90. The answer is c: Write a compound word such as *doghouse* on the board. Underline *dog*, and then *house*. Beneath the words draw a picture of a dog and a house, joined with a plus sign. Next, write another compound word and ask the class to draw the pictures in their journals. Give the students a handout with several compound words. Ask them to underline the two words, then to draw the pictures. Students will discover that compound words are composed of two distinct words that in combination mean something new but related.

91. The answer is a. Reading comprehension. Prefixes and suffixes change the meanings of the root word to which they are attached. A student who understands that *un* means "not" will be able to decipher the meanings of words such as *unwanted, unhappy,* or *unreasonable.*

92. The answer is b: Closed syllables. Closed syllables are those that end with a consonant. *At, dog, spit, duck,* and *pluck* are all examples of closed syllables.

93. The answer is b: A maze test. A maze test is a specific type of cloze test. In a cloze test, words are deleted and the reader must supply the missing words using contextual clues and vocabulary that is familiar. A maze test is a multiple-choice application of a cloze test.

94. The answer is a: Avoid idioms and slang, involve students in hands-on activities, reference students' prior knowledge, and speak slowly. Teachers of English Language Learners should not employ idioms and slang in their instruction because these informal uses of speech are likely to confuse the students. Involving students in hands-on activities such as group reading and language play makes the experience both more meaningful and more immediate. New knowledge can only be absorbed by attaching it to prior knowledge, referencing what students already know is essential. Speaking slowly to English Language Learners is important, because they are processing what is being said at a slower rate than a native speaker.

95. The answer is a: Correcting surface features such as sentence fragments, spelling, and punctuation. Editing is the final step in the writing process. The writer has already decided the ideas or events are in proper order, have been sufficiently described, and are clear. Now the writer turns her attention to surface features, "scrubbing" errors in spelling, punctuation, and syntax from the writing.

96. The answer is a: Carefully organized lessons in decoding, sight words, vocabulary, and comprehension at least three to five times a week. These mini-lessons must be extremely clear, with the parts broken down to the lowest common denominator. The more tightly interwoven and systematized the instruction, the better chance this student will have. This type of learner needs, first and foremost, instruction that has been highly organized into a system that will make sense to her. If possible, she should receive private instruction on a daily basis. The instruction needs to focus on decoding, recognizing words, reading with increasing fluency, enhancing vocabulary, and comprehension. She should be working at the Instructional level, or with texts she can read with at least 90% accuracy.

97. The answer is c: Giving a three-minute Test of Silent Contextual Reading Fluency four times a year. The student is presented with text in which spaces between words and all punctuation have been removed. The student must divide one word from another with slash marks, as in the following example:

The/little/sailboat/bobbed/so/far/in/the/distance/it/looked/like/a/toy. The more words a student accurately separates, then the higher her silent reading fluency score. Silent reading fluency can be monitored over time by giving the Test of Silent Contextual Reading Fluency (TSCRF) four times a year. A similar assessment tool is the Test of Silent Word Reading Fluency (TOSWRF), in which words of increasing complexity are given as a single, undifferentiated, and unpunctuated strand. As with the TSCRF, three minutes are given for the student to separate each word from the next.
Itwillcannotschoolbecomeagendaconsistentphilosophysuperfluous is an example of such a strand.

98. The answer is d. Haiku. Based on a Japanese form of poetry, haiku have become popular with students and teachers alike. Reading and writing haiku helps younger students become aware of syllables and helps older students learn about subtleties of vocabulary.

99. The answer is b. Confusing word or sentence order while speaking. Dyspraxic individuals do not process spoken language sequentially due to a neurological distortion. The dislocation of sounds within a word, such as vocalizing *lamp* instead of *palm*, is one indication of verbal dyspraxia.

100. The answer is b: Phonemic awareness. Vocalizing words involves arranging a series of continuous, voice, unvoiced, and stop sounds. As one sound is being uttered, the tongue and lips are already assuming the shape required by the next sound in the word. This process, which is not conscious, can distort individual sounds. One sound can slur into another, clip the end of the previous sound, or flatten or heighten a sound. For children who have difficulty hearing distinct phonemic sounds, individual instruction may be required.

Special Report: Additional Bonus Material

Due to our efforts to try to keep this book to a manageable length, we've created a link that will give you access to all of your additional bonus material.

Please visit http://www.mometrix.com/bonus948/priireadspec to access the information.